MOMS & BRAINS

Why Brain Care Matters, Especially for New Moms

MOMS & BRAINS

Why Brain Care Matters, Especially for New Moms

Prashanthi Punyakoti

This book is intended for informational purposes only and does not constitute medical advice. The author does not prescribe or recommend any technique without the guidance of a licensed healthcare professional. Any use of the information herein is solely at the reader's discretion and risk.

While this is a work of nonfiction, some names, events, and stories have been altered or dramatized for illustrative purposes. Any resemblance to actual persons, living or dead, is purely coincidental. References to public figures are based on publicly available information and are presented respectfully.

Some narratives are included to explore universal human experiences and are meant to encourage reflection, not judgment.

Published by Prashanthi

First Edition, 2025

This book is dedicated to

The Mother Nature—her quiet force shaped the soul of this book.

To the mother muses, whose generational wisdom guided me and made this journey possible in every way.

To all the mothers—past, present, and future—whose love and strength continue to shape the world.

To my parents, in-laws, and family, who have stood by me through every high and low.

To my husband, who supported me in every way throughout this journey.

Especially dedicated to the life that briefly bloomed within me—a quiet presence that left behind profound lessons.

And to my daughter, who teaches me, every day, what it means to grow, love, and begin again.

Special Dedication

To
M. Chandrasekar Sir
Retd. Chief Manager, Bank of India

Your trust in me made this possible.

Thank you for believing in me.

Contents

ACKNOWLEDGEMENTS

This book exists because of the love and guidance of the Divine Mother—Mother Nature in all her forms. I truly believe I didn't write it alone. A deeper wisdom held me through it all, especially during moments when I felt lost, tired, or unsure of where to go next.

I kept being drawn to the maternal brain—again and again—without fully understanding why at first. But the more I read, the more I felt connected, seen, and transformed. That curiosity became a path, and that path eventually led to this book.

The Divine Mother's energy revealed herself not in magical moments, but in the quiet, everyday challenges—when I lost hope or had to show up, despite the odds. She also appeared through the lens of neuroscience, pulling me deeper into the mysteries of the maternal brain. And as I explored its depths, I realized something beautiful: she is present in every facet of life.

The more I came to understand the maternal brain and its divine nature, the more I saw that science is not separate from spirituality—it is simply another way to experience her presence.

This book is a testament to that connection. I hope it helps every new mom feel seen, supported, and reminded that the journey you're on is sacred—both scientifically and spiritually.

Authors note:

This book is a blend of real experiences, inner reflections, and stories—some drawn from life, others shaped to carry a deeper message. Along the way, I've mentioned public figures and events that influenced me. My intention is not to judge anyone, but to explore how our outer world affects our inner journey. Where needed, names or details have been changed to honor privacy and keep the focus on the lesson, not the person.

May these stories spark awareness, not conclusions—and may they gently guide you toward your own truth.

FOREWORD

The birth of a child is celebrated with joy, rituals, and congratulations. Yet, in that very moment, another birth quietly unfolds — the birth of a mother.

As a pediatrician and a mother myself, I am privileged to witness the earliest chapters of many mother–child stories. From the first cry to the first step, we closely monitor a newborn's growth and milestones, but rarely pause to acknowledge the profound physiological and emotional shifts taking place within the mother.

Pregnancy and childbirth do not simply change a woman's body — they reshape her hormones, her brain, her instincts, and her identity. Behind every infant is a woman navigating sleep deprivation, hormonal fluctuations, emotional vulnerability, and the immense responsibility of nurturing new life. This phase — though natural — can feel disorienting and overwhelming. Yet, it is deeply powerful.

The early mother–child bond is not only emotional; it is neurological. Through touch, eye contact, voice, and emotional presence, the child begins to grow and respond to maternal stimulation. These early interactions build intricate neuronal connections — what we call neuroplasticity. Emotional regulation begins during this time, and maternal interaction plays a crucial role in shaping these networks and, ultimately, the child's future.

But this process is not one-sided — it happens both ways.

As the child grows, the mother evolves too. Motherhood is not only about raising a child; it is also about the reorganization of a woman's inner world. Yet, this transition is often overlooked due to a lack of awareness about the importance of a mother's mental well-being.

A strong and calm mother can provide a nurturing environment for the child. Therefore, caring for a mother is not a luxury — it is essential.

As a close friend of the author, I have seen not only her dedication to this book but also her deep empathy for mothers navigating this beautiful yet fragile phase. This book gives voice to what so many mothers feel but are unable to express. She beautifully connects scientific understanding with real-life experience, making complex ideas easy to understand.

This book reassures mothers that growth often hides within moments of doubt and confusion. It honors the sacred reciprocity of motherhood — as the mother shapes the child, the child reshapes the mother's spirit. It also gently guides mothers toward practical coping approaches.

I hope every mother who opens this book feels seen, understood, and inspired to nurture her own mind while caring for her child.

This book will be a meaningful gift for any woman stepping into motherhood.

— Dr. Udaya Keerthi
Pediatrician & Mother

PREFACE

In August 2016, on an ordinary day, as the clock struck noon, my husband headed off to work. I lingered around the house, tidied up, grabbed some lunch, and then reclined on the bed, weighed down by a heavy sense of grief.

All of a sudden, a faint pain surfaced in the lower right side of my stomach. At first, it was easy to dismiss, but with each passing moment, it intensified. Realizing something was wrong, I called my husband, barely able to speak through the groans. Within minutes, the discomfort escalated, leading to relentless vomiting.

Overwhelmed, I collapsed on the bathroom floor, incapable of moving. At the ER, I emptied two more buckets of bodily fluids. I looked like a cadaver, drained of every ounce of my strength. And yet, my biggest worry wasn't for me—it was for the tiny, seven-week-old heart that had just started beating inside me.

As I lay in that hospital bed, vivid memories came rushing back. They transported me to another hospital bed, months earlier, in March 2016. Back then, I was happily married and 22 weeks pregnant. It was supposed to be a routine scan. But as the doctor slid the probe across my belly, the room filled with unbearable silence. When I looked at him, hoping for reassurance, he spoke the words that shattered me: the baby was gone.

I stared at the gray image on the screen, unable to believe what I saw. The baby was there, but there was no life. How could that be possible? It was inside me—I could feel it. But the truth was undeniable. My colorful life turned gray that day. That moment left a lasting scar on my soul that no one can erase.

While carrying the weight of that trauma, I was also managing a job transfer, a new city, and mismatched schedules with my husband. There wasn't even space to grieve.

As I drifted back from those memories, a nurse walked in and told me I had food poisoning—probably from something I ate or medication taken at the wrong time. Two days later, I was discharged, only to be re-admitted with another red flag. I was diagnosed with placenta previa, which put me on bed rest for the rest of my pregnancy. Overnight, my fast-paced life turned into a slow-motion movie.

With life rolling out a red carpet of challenges, I stepped into motherhood—uncertain and unprepared for what lay ahead. I was still drowning in the grief of losing one baby while raising another. I felt everything at once: delighted yet depressed, loved yet rejected, overwhelmed yet responsible. Fear gripped me every time I tried to bond with my baby. That fear slowly morphed into anxiety, depression, and hypertension.

I lost my health. I left my job. I lost my financial independence, my emotional balance, and my sense of identity. I hit what felt like rock bottom. I tried starting a business from home, but it failed miserably. Financial strain tightened its grip, emotional overwhelm took over, and isolation became my reality.

On the outside, I looked like a new mother. Inside, I was quietly breaking.

And yet… something unexpected saved me—brain care—and it helped me rebuild my life piece by piece. After my child was born, I came to know about something rarely spoken about: maternal brain health—what people casually call "mom brain." It's the biological transition phase into motherhood, known as matrescence—similar to adolescence, when a woman's brain rewires at a cellular level.

That realization changed everything. I began to research, journal, and absorb everything I could—TED Talks, podcasts, scientific studies, and wisdom from ancient traditions. I integrated neuroscience, mindfulness, meditation, and powerful visualization practices. And that led me on the most transformative inward journey of my life.

Slowly, I didn't just bounce back—I rewired, rediscovered, and rebuilt myself—emotionally, physically, financially, and even spiritually.

That journey opened my eyes to something profound: Motherhood is the most underrated transition phase in our society.

But when women are aware, supported, and guided properly, it can become the greatest superpower of their lives. We become more confident, more focused, more balanced, more abundant.

Somewhere along the way, under layers of conditioned beliefs—rules, restrictions, and taboos—we forget who we truly are. We wear labels, follow scripts, and accept suffering as normal. But it isn't. There is a way to clear that brain fog. That understanding came after years of struggle and deep inner work—and it gave birth to this book.

This is not just a book. It's a reflection of my transformation—and an invitation to yours. Because every mother deserves brain care—not as a luxury, but as a necessity.

Inside, you'll find the stories, science, and tools that helped me reclaim my mental clarity, inner calm, and true potential. My hope is that it gives you the same clarity and strength it gave me.

If there's one thing my journey has taught me, it's this: when you care for your brain and focus within, you don't just survive—you rise beyond.

Undoubtedly, the journey had its share of ups and downs, but the invaluable end result made every twist and turn worthwhile.

INTRODUCTION

The world around us is changing rapidly. With shifting socioeconomic conditions, relentless work demands, and the pressures of daily life, self-care often feels like a luxury we can no longer afford. For women, especially those navigating pregnancy and motherhood, this reality can feel overwhelming.

Have you ever felt like self-care is a luxury you can't afford amidst the relentless demands of motherhood? Parenting, once a shared community experience, has transformed into a solitary journey for many, particularly in the era of nuclear families.

It's often said, "It takes a village to raise a child." But what happens when that village isn't there—or when it's more stressful than supportive? Family dynamics can sometimes add to the strain. Well-meaning loved ones often offer advice, but differing opinions on parenting can overwhelm a mom who's already doubting her instincts.

Have you ever wondered why parenting advice never seems to work?

Because parenting doesn't happen as an external instruction—it unfolds as a side effect of who you are at a subconscious level. That's why it's so important to become conscious of your subconscious patterns.

The lack of a robust support system leaves many women juggling motherhood alone, often at the expense of their own well-being. Even with access to daycare or external help, the anxiety lingers, and the questions never stop:

- "If I work, does that mean I'm unavailable as a mother?"
- "If I don't work, will I be seen as lazy or unambitious?"
- "Am I doing enough for my child?"
- "Will my decisions today ruin my child's future?"

These thoughts play on repeat, creating a cycle of guilt, anxiety, and self-doubt. But what if I told you there's a way to break free from this cycle? What if thriving as a mother, even with limited external support, is not just possible but achievable? This book offers a solution you may not have considered—***taking care of your brain***.

Your brain isn't just another organ; it's your command center, shaping every thought, emotion, and action. It has the power to shape your world and your experience of motherhood. When nurtured and cared for, it becomes your most powerful ally, giving you clarity, resilience, and adaptability. Yet, brain health is often overlooked, particularly for mothers, despite the profound changes the brain undergoes during pregnancy and motherhood.

Have you ever wondered why maternal instincts don't always arise the way they're supposed to?

It's because the modern mother's brain is often hijacked by constant survival demands—juggling between ancient biological wiring and the pressures of today's fast-paced world. These overlapping struggles can mute the very instincts that nature designed to guide her.

Motherhood is more than a physical journey—it is a profound neurological transformation. During pregnancy and beyond, a woman's brain undergoes significant changes, enhancing her capacity for empathy, resilience, and bonding. But this same period also leaves her more vulnerable to stress, anxiety, and trauma. Sadly, in the relentless pursuit of meeting societal and cultural expectations, many women neglect their own mental and emotional needs, leaving their brains overburdened and undernourished.

This book offers solutions for making self-care possible despite the challenges of motherhood and unlocking your true potential.

Here's what makes this book unique: It's not just about motherhood; it's about understanding the incredible changes happening in your brain and using that knowledge to transform your life. It goes beyond surface-level advice, offering science-backed tools and insights to help you thrive.

Through these pages, you'll discover:

- What happens to your brain during pregnancy and motherhood.
- The unique challenges new moms face.
- How stress and trauma affect brain health.
- The myths surrounding brain care and why it's often neglected.
- A transformational journey of hope and resilience, rooted in my personal experiences.
- Tools and techniques like meditation, visualization, and time and energy management to help you thrive.

This isn't just a book; it's a roadmap to reclaiming your life. It's about moving from survival mode to thriving, from feeling overwhelmed to feeling empowered. With step-by-step guidance and practical hacks, you'll learn how to nourish your brain, manage your energy, and embrace a holistic lifestyle that transforms not only your motherhood journey but your entire life.

Motherhood doesn't have to mean losing yourself. When you care for your brain, you create a foundation of strength, clarity, and joy that radiates through every aspect of your life.

It's time to stop asking, "Am I doing enough?" and start asking, "What does my brain need to help me thrive?"
This book will show you how to tap into that power—because every mother deserves to not just survive but to thrive. Only a mother who is happy inside can radiate that joy outside. A happy mother means a happy baby, a happy family, and, in turn, a happier society.

Let's begin this journey together. It's time to care for the masterpiece within you, to rediscover your strength, and to create a life filled with joy, abundance, and fulfillment. Motherhood is not just about nurturing a new life; it's about nurturing your own. And it all begins with your brain.

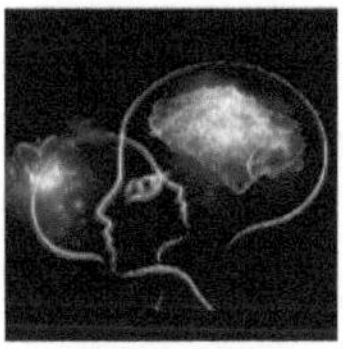

CHAPTER 1

WELCOME MOMMY BRAIN

Mayuri was tense, pacing outside the operating room. Her clothes were stained with blood and tears streamed down her face as she prayed. Her heart was racing, her breath was ragged. Her husband, standing by, tried to calm her, though he was just as shocked and worried. Moments later, the doctor emerged. Pulling down his mask, he smiled and said, "Nothing to worry about. It's a small injury. A few stitches were needed on his forehead. You can take him home in two hours." Only then did Mayuri find some relief. She hurried inside to see her two-year-old son lying on the bed. He had suffered an accidental injury to his forehead, losing a lot of blood. The cut was so deep that he had cried and fainted.

A few days later, I visited Mayuri's home to check on her son. His stitches had been removed, and he was already back to playing.

"Welcome! It's been a long time since we met," said Mayuri as she welcomed me into her home.

Mayuri seemed happy, relaxed, and content, a stark contrast to the person that she was before. Mayuri was an ambitious woman with goals and dreams. But she was also anxious and depressed all the time.

"You seem very happy," I exclaimed.

"I'm having the best time ever," she smiled.

I was glad for her. The Mayuri I had known was different. Her life had always been a juggling act between tradition and ambition. Raised in a small village within a large family, she was surrounded by the domestic life her culture expected of women. Though she was ambitious, she always believed her future would be confined to the kitchen after marriage. But her mother, who had spent countless hours in that very kitchen, dreamed of more for her daughter. She saw how other women who worked outside the home gained respect and independence.

Mayuri was reluctant to leave her family; however, she left her family and pursued her studies, becoming strong, self-reliant, and confident. At a young age, she landed a job with a multinational company. Through hard work, she earned both money and recognition, traveling the world as a representative of her company. She married a colleague and built a successful career.

Despite her achievements, Mayuri was not truly happy. Ten years into her marriage, she still hadn't conceived, while everyone around her—friends, colleagues, and cousins—were raising children. Mayuri had always imagined her future with a loving husband and kids, so the absence of children weighed heavily on her. She tried everything to get pregnant. She approached many doctors, prayed to the gods, and tried every possible remedy, but nothing worked. Left with little hope, she carried on with her life.

Years later, during a family function, Mayuri felt light-headed and fainted. A doctor attending the event said it was due to stress and advised her to rest. While resting, a friend suggested she take a pregnancy test. Mayuri was reluctant, having faced disappointment hundreds of times before. But when she took the test, she was astonished to see two red lines. She immediately called her husband. Still in disbelief, they rushed to the hospital for confirmation. As they waited for the results, I met Mayuri. We were both first-time expectant mothers, and we quickly bonded, sharing our thoughts on the journey ahead.

With a six-figure income, a successful career, a loving husband, and a luxurious lifestyle, Mayuri seemed to have it all—at least, that's what I thought before I understood the meaning of true success. While Mayuri welcomed her baby boy, I was still recovering from the trauma of my earlier unsuccessful pregnancy.

For her, becoming a mother brought immense joy, but within four months, her years of waiting broke her heart. She had to return to work. The thought of leaving her son made Mayuri anxious and filled her with worry. Unable to stay home, she hired a nanny after thorough screening. However, she couldn't focus on work. Her mind was constantly on her son, and when she had to travel overseas for a two-day trip, it became unbearable. Upon returning, she resigned.

When her husband asked why, she shared a story that had shaken her. On her flight back, she met a single mother traveling with her 13-year-old son for the first time. The woman explained that her career had kept her from bonding with her child. Now that she had more time, she was trying to make up for the lost years. This struck a chord with Mayuri. She had waited so long for a child, and now she felt she was missing out on the precious time she had longed for. Though she had achieved so much, Mayuri realized that nothing mattered more than being present for her son.

What Mayuri didn't fully realize was that her strong urge to be with her son wasn't just triggered by the conversation she had on the flight. It went much deeper.

The intense pull she felt toward her son was part of something bigger—her brain was going through neurological changes that all new mothers experience. Research has shown that pregnancy and motherhood lead to structural and functional changes in the brain, particularly in areas responsible for social cognition, emotional regulation, and bonding (Hoekzema et al., 2017). These changes enhance a mother's ability to connect with, protect, and prioritize her child, often without her conscious awareness.

Mayuri's story illustrates the profound biological and emotional shifts, showing how the maternal brain is wired to nurture and protect, even when a mother isn't fully aware of the transformation happening within her.

Kavya's story is another powerful example of just how far a mother can go for her child.

Kavya was a 53-year-old woman who passed away recently. I attended her funeral with my friend Megha. Kavya's life had been far from ordinary. Married young, at 16, to an addict, she had two children. When her daughter, Kiran, was just a year old, her husband came home drunk and threw her during a fight. Kiran hit her head against a wall and never recovered. Though her body grew, her brain remained that of a one-year-old for the rest of her life. Kavya was only 18 when this tragedy happened, but she vowed never to abandon her daughter.

Despite the overwhelming challenges, she fought for Kiran, shielding her from the cruelty of others. Years turned into decades, but her devotion never wavered. Science tells us that when a mother cares for her child, especially under difficult circumstances, her brain adapts in ways that strengthen resilience and deepen attachment. The circuits in her brain responsible for caregiving, particularly in the amygdala and prefrontal cortex—become more active, reinforcing her ability to nurture even under stress (Swain et al., 2011). This could explain how Kavya, a young girl, found the strength to devote her life to her child.

Kiran passed away at 35, and within a year, Kavya followed—as if her life's purpose had been fulfilled. Her story reminds us that the bond between a mother and child isn't just emotional—it is wired into the brain. Studies have shown that the pain of losing a loved one, especially a child, activates the same areas of the brain as physical pain (Eisenberger, 2012). Perhaps that's why her body could no longer carry on.

At the funeral, while everyone mourned and remembered Kavya's remarkable patience and resilience, I recalled a haunting incident that happened back in 2004.

One morning, our entire neighborhood was shaken by the discovery of a newborn baby in a sewage canal. The mother had abandoned her child, leaving the baby to die. I can still see the tiny foot of that baby floating above the water. The image has stayed with me all these years, and so has the question: How could a mother abandon her child?

While mothers like Kavya stand as examples of sacrifice, child abandonment is also increasing. It's a stark contrast—some mothers will give up everything for their child, while others feel no connection at all. Lost in deep thought and heavy emotions, I left the funeral.

After the funeral, Megha and I returned home. Reflecting on Kavya's life, we thought that Kavya's strength was nothing short of extraordinary, and it shows the unimaginable depth of maternal sacrifice, yet it's a path no mother should have to walk. Kavya's dedication and sacrifice underscore the deep-rooted maternal instincts that arise during this period, driven by profound changes in the brain.

While Kavya's journey was so intense, Megha's was no less remarkable. Born into a conservative family with strict, superstitious beliefs, she wasn't allowed to pursue education beyond high school. But Megha had dreams. She wanted to make a name for herself in theater arts. At 19, she left home and moved to the city. With her striking looks, she quickly found work in advertisements and modeling. At the peak of her career, she fell in love with a photographer and got married in secret, knowing that being a married model would hurt her chances in the industry. But everything changed when she got pregnant. As the baby grew inside, her chances as a model diminished, and Megha's career came to a halt. When she stopped earning, her husband left. Alone and pregnant, Megha faced her journey head-on.

After years of hard work, raising her child on her own, Megha eventually grew stronger and started her own business. She was one of the strongest women I knew, always moving forward no matter how difficult life became. Her story is proof that the transition into motherhood isn't just about having a baby—it's about the rewiring of a woman's brain, shaping her thoughts, instincts, and identity in ways she never expected.

The stories of Mayuri, Kavya, and Megha show us how becoming a mother can change a person's life in deep and emotional ways. These personal experiences highlight the intense shifts new moms go through. But there's more to it than just feelings and daily challenges.

What makes such a big difference in a woman's life? Why do some moms dive deeply into parenting, while others find it tough or even step away? The answer lies in what happens inside the brain. Scientists have discovered that a mother's brain literally changes during this time. Understanding these brain changes helps explain why the transition into motherhood feels so profound and why these experiences are common to new moms. Now, let's look at what happens in the brain to create these shifts.

Mommy Brain: The Brain's Rebirth

Luna was a friendly dog who always loved her human family. She was playful, gentle, and adored being around people. But when Luna became a mother, everything changed. One afternoon, while her puppies were just a few weeks old, a neighbor's dog wandered too close. In an instant, Luna, who was once so calm, transformed into a fierce protector. Her deep growls and strong stance sent the other dog running before it could come near her puppies. Her family was astonished by this sudden change; it was as though a switch had flipped the moment she became a mother. Luna's maternal aggression, a deep-rooted survival instinct, came out in full force to ensure the safety of her babies.

This phenomenon is not unique to Luna. Almost every animal displays protective behavior once they become parents. A mother bear will aggressively defend her cubs if she feels threatened, and birds, like geese, will hiss and chase away anything that comes too close to their nest. We often hear stories of human mothers performing extraordinary feats, like lifting a car to protect their baby. These behaviors are a natural part of evolution, a survival mechanism passed down by Mother Nature to ensure the protection and continuation of the species.

Scientists have found that this heightened sense of protectiveness is driven by changes in the brain, particularly in the amygdala—the region responsible for processing threats. During motherhood, the amygdala becomes more sensitive, increasing a mother's vigilance and enhancing her ability to detect and respond to potential dangers. This biological transformation is what allows a calm and gentle mother to instantly turn into a fierce protector when her child is at risk (Lonstein & Gammie, 2002).

But aggression isn't the only maternal behavior that surfaces after birth. Nursing, nurturing, keeping their young warm, grooming, and maintaining hygiene all become priorities for mothers once their babies arrive. Have you ever wondered why you're always worried about your baby's well-being, or why you spend so much time cleaning and sterilizing everything? Or why do you suddenly feel the need to baby-proof the entire house? Maybe you've noticed you're forgetting simple things, like where you left your car keys or phone. Sometimes it's even hard to follow a conversation or make decisions without feeling overwhelmed. These are common experiences for new moms.

This shift happens because your brain physically changes after giving birth, becoming fully focused on your baby's survival. The so-called "Mommy Brain" is born alongside your baby, and it changes everything. It's not like your regular brain anymore—Its only goal is to protect your baby at all costs. Mommy Brain makes you zoom in on tiny threats like germs, while also zooming out to think about your baby's entire future.

I remember how much time I spent sterilizing everything—way more than I ever did in my biotech lab during college! I even missed that old abandoned autoclave (a machine we used to sterilize things under high pressure) from our lab. I found myself doing things I'd never done before, like planning for the future and trying to follow healthy habits for my baby.

Normally, I'm just a regular person—someone who procrastinates, avoids routines, and rarely thinks too far ahead. I used to live without a clear purpose. But after having my baby, it felt like someone else had taken over my mind. I wasn't in charge anymore.

It reminded me of the movie *Ratatouille*—except instead of a rat controlling me from the outside, it's the Mommy Brain inside, taking over my regular brain, which I like to call my "Muggle Brain." The Muggle Brain is just my usual self—lazy, carefree, and always putting things off.

In her book, *The Female Brain*, neuropsychiatrist Louann Brizendine, M.D., explains that the brain is *"primed and marinated"* during gestation, rewiring itself at a cellular level to prepare for the upcoming event: motherhood. The birth of a baby also brings the birth of the mother's new brain, fully focused on protecting her child (Brizendine, 2006).

In general, even a small brain seizure can completely transform someone's personality. For mothers, these changes are on an immense scale, reshaping not just their physiology but also profoundly influencing who they are. Your brain is preparing you for all kinds of challenges that come with the baby—whether it's sleepless nights, reading your baby's cues, or finding new ways to balance responsibilities and priorities.

Researchers call this ability of the brain to change "neuroplasticity." This flexibility helps you adapt to your new role, even though it can feel overwhelming at times. Studies confirm that motherhood triggers significant neuroplastic changes in the brain, especially in areas involved in learning, memory, and emotional regulation (Kim, 2016). These changes allow mothers to develop new skills, strengthen emotional resilience, and enhance their ability to bond with their babies.

If you are a new mom and you've heard others say, "You're not the same person I used to know," they're probably right. Your brain has changed, and while this transformation is a testament to the brain's adaptive power, not all changes will feel good. The brain's rewiring, coupled with hormonal, physical, emotional, and psychological shifts, can be overwhelming.

You may recall how dramatically your behavior changed during adolescence, when you were labeled rebellious or daring. If those teenage years felt intense, then brace yourself for the rollercoaster ride of the transition phase of motherhood, often called **"Matrescence"** by scientists. Just like puberty, this transition comes with intense emotional, psychological, and biological shifts (Barba-Müller et al., 2019).

Although it's not a commonly used term, becoming aware of this transition phase helps new mothers recognize that their experiences are a normal part of this profound life change.

Matrescence

Motherhood doesn't happen overnight. Just as adolescence involves significant changes in hormones, the brain, and the body during the transition to adulthood, matrescence involves similar changes as a woman adjusts to her new role as a mother. The term *"Matrescence"* was introduced by anthropologist, Dana Raphael in the 1970s (Raphael, 1973).

To better understand the changes a mother goes through during matrescence, think of it like renovating your house. Just as a home renovation involves tearing down old walls and building new ones, your brain goes through a similar "remodeling" process when you become a mom. This mental makeover helps you adapt to the new demands of motherhood. Let's take a closer look at how this transformation unfolds.

Picture this: you decide to renovate your house—replacing the kitchen, bedrooms, and bathrooms, all while a new metro line is being built on your usual route to work. Suddenly, everything feels out of place. Your bed isn't where it used to be, and you can't find your kitchen items to make even a simple cup of coffee. Tasks that used to be quick and easy now take much longer.

Then, as you step outside, your smooth commute has turned into a construction zone. The streets are filled with traffic, dust, and heavy machinery, and what used to be a 20-minute drive is now a bumpy, tiring journey. By the time you reach work, you're already exhausted. And imagine, this chaotic routine becomes your new normal for the next few years. You know the renovation and metro line will eventually make things better, but right now, it's overwhelming.

Just like that renovation, motherhood is a process of rebuilding. It's messy, exhausting, and uncomfortable, but deep down, these changes are laying the foundation for something better. Your brain starts to reorganize itself, forming new neural connections and pathways to meet the demands of caring for a newborn and learning the skills needed for parenting (Orchard et al., 2023).

It's as if your brain, like a city, is laying down the "metro line" of motherhood, building a new system for the future. But in doing so, your current priorities get reshuffled. While this transformation will eventually support you as a parent, the journey can feel overwhelming and confusing.

During this phase, your hormones surge, your priorities shift, and your body goes through changes. You become someone you've never met before—a version of yourself that's still taking shape. Psychiatrists now recognize that this process is not just a hormonal shift but a profound psychological transformation that can bring both growth and struggle.

In her TED Talk, psychiatrist Alexandra Sacks describes matrescence as a period of identity reconstruction, where women experience both joy and grief as they navigate their new roles (Sacks.2018).

As we've discussed, becoming a mother brings significant changes to your brain and how you see yourself. While these changes can help you care for your baby, they also come with challenges that go beyond your personal experiences.

New moms often face outside pressures, like societal expectations, financial worries, and emotional struggles, which can make this transition even harder (Athan, 2024). The way your brain adjusts internally is also based on how these outside factors affect you, creating a unique situation for each mother.

In the next chapter, we'll look more closely at these challenges, including not just the biological changes but also the societal and emotional pressures that can complicate motherhood. By understanding and addressing these issues, you can better handle this exciting yet overwhelming time more confidently.

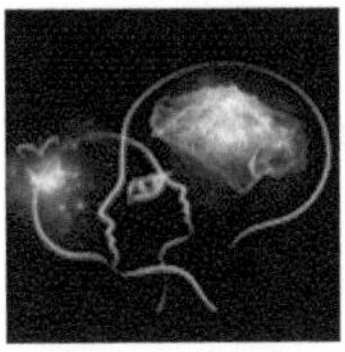

CHAPTER 2

MOMMY BRAIN STRUGGLES

Motherhood is both rewarding and overwhelming. It brings challenges, from sleepless nights to the constant demands of caring for a newborn. It's no surprise that many moms feel like their brains are in overdrive. On top of that, many struggle with an identity shift, questioning who they were before and who they are now as a mother.

Smitha was a successful lawyer who always prided herself on her sharp memory and her ability to multitask. She handled high-profile cases, juggling client meetings, courtroom appearances, and endless emails without breaking a sweat.

But after her daughter was born, everything suddenly changed. She began forgetting simple things—like the names of her most important clients or whether she had responded to a crucial email.

"It's like my brain has been hijacked," she joked, trying to laugh it off, but deep down, the frustration was real.

She adored her daughter more than anything, yet couldn't shake the unsettling feeling that a part of her was slipping away. How could she love her child so much but feel like she was losing herself at the same time?

Nandini, a first-time mother and a natural planner, had always kept her life organized. From managing her career to planning every detail of her day, she was always in control. But the arrival of her baby turned her structured world upside down.

"There are days I don't know what I'm doing," she admitted, her voice heavy with exhaustion.

"It's like I'm constantly in a fog, juggling everything but never really catching up."

She had expected sleepless nights, but what caught her off guard was the mental fog, the constant feeling of being overwhelmed, and the emotional toll it all took on her. She often found herself wondering why no one had told her about these feelings before she became a mother.

Then there's Christine, a mother of two who has been through this journey more than once. She recalls how, after her first child, she felt a part of her identity slowly fade away.

"It's like I had to rebuild myself, piece by piece. I wasn't just Christine anymore—I was a mother, and that meant something entirely different."

The process was painful, yet beautiful, as she learned to embrace the new version of herself. She missed the carefree woman she used to be.

These stories are far from unique. All over the world, women experience this mental and emotional shift when they enter motherhood. What many don't realize is that these feelings aren't just emotional; they're deeply biological. Your brain is rewiring itself, adapting to the new demands of motherhood. It's a transformation that affects every part of your being.

For me, as a single window operator in the bank, I was used to deal with countless customers every day, solving different types of problems and responding to requests without hesitation. Communication was never an issue. Whether it was explaining banking policies or helping someone with a transaction, I could do it all with ease.

But after my daughter was born, something shifted. I struggled to find words for even the simplest conversations, even with my husband. It was as if the part of my brain that handled communication had gone on vacation.

Scientific research supports these experiences. A meta-analysis by Davies et al. (2025) found a significant decline in cognitive function in pregnant women compared to non-pregnant women, particularly in attention, memory, and executive function.

Another study by Davies et al. (2021) found that pregnant women exhibited impairments in memory and language skills, particularly in naming, which were attributed to hormonal and physiological changes. Additionally, research by Zheng et al. (2018) in *Frontiers in Psychology* revealed decreased spontaneous neural activity in postpartum women, especially in the prefrontal cortex, which correlated with impaired cognitive function, further reinforcing the biological basis of "mommy brain."

Much like Smitha, Nandini, and Christine, many new moms face similar struggles. Here are some of the most common challenges mothers fight every day.

Most common challenges new moms face:

- **Identity Shift:** Becoming a mom can feel like losing yourself. Balancing who you were before with the new role can be confusing.
- **Physical Changes:** Pregnancy and childbirth cause physical changes like recovery from labor, hormonal shifts, and fatigue—which affect both mind and body.
- **Emotional Ups and Downs:** Your emotions can swing wildly after having a baby, from happiness to stress or sadness.
- **Lack of Sleep:** Sleep deprivation from caring for a newborn makes everything harder, including coping with daily challenges.
- **Increased Responsibilities:** Looking after a baby is a full-time job—feeding, changing diapers, soothing, and constant attention.
- **Relationship Changes:** How you relate to your partner, friends, and family can shift, sometimes causing tension.
- **Social and Cultural Expectations:** Society often pressures moms to be perfect, which can lead to guilt if things don't go as planned.
- **Feeling Isolated:** Caring for a baby can limit social time, leaving new moms feeling lonely.
- **Financial Stress:** Raising a baby can strain finances, especially if work situations change.

- **Lack of Help:** Not all moms have enough support, which can make motherhood feel overwhelming, especially for nuclear families.
- **Doubt and Uncertainty:** Many new moms doubt themselves, wondering if they're doing things right.
- **Brain and Hormone Changes:** "Mom brain" is real—hormonal changes can affect memory, mood, and thinking clearly.

Addressing these challenges requires a combination of education, support, and self-care. Providing new moms with information about matrescence, encouraging open communication, and fostering strong support networks can help ease the transition and promote well-being during this critical period.

It's important to understand that while all new moms go through matrescence—a natural and temporary process of adapting to motherhood—some may experience postpartum depression (PPD), a more serious condition that requires treatment. While matrescence feels like an identity shift or an emotional roller coaster, PPD can bring persistent sadness, hopelessness, and a disconnection from your baby.

If you suspect you have postpartum depression, consult your doctor immediately. It's important to get help when:

- You feel sad or hopeless most of the time.
- You have trouble bonding with the baby.
- You have thoughts of harming yourself or the baby.

- You experience severe mood swings or intense anger.
- You have trouble sleeping, even when your baby is asleep.
- You feel guilty or worthless.
- These feelings last more than two weeks or get worse over time.

A Mother's Unseen Challenges

While new moms face numerous challenges, there are deeper, often unseen factors influencing their mental health—turning an already tough journey into a more chaotic one.

The Lack of Support Systems

A strong support system is essential for a new mother's mental well-being. While partners and family members can help ease the burden, their absence often leaves moms feeling isolated and overwhelmed.

Beyond family, the lack of supportive work policies, adequate postpartum care, and accessible resources can push many mothers into a battle with feelings of inadequacy and burnout.

The Pressure to "Do It All"

Societal expectations to balance work, parenting, and financial responsibilities add even more pressure. From managing households to excelling at work, the expectation to "do it all" often makes moms feel like failures when they inevitably fall short of impossible standards.

As if these age-old challenges weren't enough, modern mothers now face additional hurdles that intensify the pressure.

The Social Media Influence

We're all guilty of doom-scrolling on social media, especially when we're exhausted and seeking comfort. In a world where social media influencers showcase picture-perfect lives, it's easy for new moms to feel like they're falling short.

I once followed Ruby Franke, a popular influencer—also called a "momfluencer"—whose YouTube channel, *8 Passengers*, had millions of followers. As a mother of six, she seemed to embody the image of a supermom. I found myself trying to follow her advice, thinking, *if she can do it, so can I.*

Later, widely reported news revealed that her strict parenting style had spiraled into serious legal consequences, including her arrest on child abuse charges. Her story underscored the troubling gap between the polished images we see online and the more complex, often painful, realities behind the screen.

Ruby Franke's case is just one example of how social media can distort reality — influencing how new moms perceive themselves and their parenting.

The Perfection Trap

Another example is Veda, an influencer obsessed with perfection. From pristine homes to flawless kids, her social media feed showcased an ideal life.

But behind the scenes, she was drowning in debt from trying to keep up appearances. She eventually shut down her accounts, but the damage was done. Her curated life left many moms feeling like they could never measure up.

While some influencers openly share their struggles, creating supportive communities, many present only polished highlights. This fuels feelings of inadequacy, especially for moms without strong support systems.

Key Factors Influencing Mommy Brain

- **Unrealistic Standards:** Social media's highlight reels lead new moms to unfairly compare themselves to idealized portrayals of motherhood, sparking stress and self-doubt.
- **Information Overload:** The overwhelming amount of parenting advice online can leave moms confused about what's right for their baby.
- **Distraction:** Constant connectivity makes it hard for new moms to stay present, distracting them from bonding with their child.

The Pressure of Pop Culture

Celebrity culture and media add yet another layer of unrealistic expectations. From red-carpet-ready postpartum looks to effortless parenting portrayals, the gap between reality and these glamorized versions of motherhood deepens feelings of inadequacy.

The Good Mother/Bad Mother Syndrome

Rigid societal standards create an internal battle for moms, making them constantly question if they're doing enough. This tug-of-war between being a "good" or "bad" mom often leads to feelings of shame and guilt.

The Impact of Mom Guilt

Mom guilt takes a heavy toll on mental health, self-esteem, and the mother-child bond. When it takes over, moms may struggle to stay present, missing precious moments of connection with their child.

- **Self-Doubt:** Moms constantly second-guess their parenting choices, gradually losing confidence.
- **Perfectionism:** The pressure to be the perfect mom leads to burnout and exhaustion.
- **Comparisons:** Looking at other moms' lives—especially on social media—fuels feelings of inadequacy.

- **Judgment Fear:** Many moms worry they'll be judged, adding more stress to their already full plate.

How to Cope with Mom Guilt

- **Set Realistic Expectations:** Understand that perfection is a myth—every mom has good and bad days.
- **Self-Compassion:** Be kind to yourself. It's okay to struggle; motherhood is tough.
- **Limit Social Media:** Reducing time on social media helps avoid unhealthy comparisons.
- **Seek Support:** Connecting with other moms or speaking to a therapist can ease feelings of isolation.
- **Celebrate Small Wins:** Recognize and cherish every little achievement—motherhood is full of small victories.

If these issues aren't addressed, they can lead to serious consequences—significantly impacting a mother's brain health and overall well-being. All of these challenges can add up and result in chronic stress.

While short-term (acute) stress can help protect you in dangerous situations, chronic stress, which persists over time, can severely affect your life—and most importantly, your bond with your baby.

It's hard to remain unaffected when you're constantly bombarded with information and facing the pressure of unrealistic expectations. I, too, fell into the trap.

Surrounded by "super moms" on social media, with their perfect lives and flawless routines, I couldn't help but feel inadequate, like I wasn't enough. No matter how hard I tried, I felt like I was failing. I tried to follow every trendy parenting method, bought all the right baby products, and followed every piece of advice on health and nutrition. While some of it helped, deep down, I always felt I was falling short.

On top of that, I was stuck in my own personal struggles—leaving my job, dealing with financial stress, and facing many other challenges. I was sabotaging my relationships too. Even though I researched and journaled obsessively, it felt like no matter what I did, I couldn't shake off the weight on my chest. The pressure was suffocating, and I didn't even realize how much stress I was piling on myself until I couldn't sleep at night, not because of the baby, but because of my own racing thoughts. I was under chronic stress without realizing how it was affecting my body and my ability to bond with my baby.

Research shows that stress can interfere with a mother's ability to bond with her baby. For instance, in one study, stressed mother rats displayed poor bonding by ignoring their young, while calmer mothers exhibited nurturing behavior (Champagne & Meaney, 2006). Similarly, human studies have found that chronic stress can lower oxytocin levels, making it harder for mothers to bond with their babies (Feldman et al., 2007). This illustrates the profound impact of stress on maternal instincts.

It all comes down to the brain's chemicals—dopamine, the reward hormone, and oxytocin, the love hormone. These hormones are essential for bonding, rewarding you for caring for your child and making the experience deeply fulfilling.

In fact, these hormones are released by the brain and are the reason that becoming a mother can feel like such a rewarding experience. However, when stress lowers these hormone levels, it becomes challenging to connect with our babies. I often wonder about mothers raising their children in war-torn areas—how does constant stress affect their ability to bond?

A Life-Changing Encounter

At my breaking point, I realized I couldn't make this overwhelming journey alone. Deep down, I knew I needed help, but the fear of judgment or getting caught in blame games held me back from sharing my struggles with anyone.

One day, I finally opened up to my trusted friend Megha. I poured out my frustrations and asked how she managed to handle her own challenges without crumbling under them.

Megha listened patiently, her eyes filled with understanding, then gave a knowing smile.

"I know exactly what you need," she said.

"You're going to get all the answers—not just for your journaling but for your mental well-being too," she added, her words offering a glimmer of hope.

A week later, Megha called me early in the morning.

"Today's the day," she announced with excitement. "I'm taking you to meet someone. Be ready in an hour." Before hanging up, she mentioned, "Her name is Aditi."

From the way Megha spoke about Aditi, I pictured an older, wise woman—probably in her 50s. I couldn't help but wonder if Megha was exaggerating. But with nothing to lose, I agreed to go.

Looking back now, I can say without a doubt that it was one of the best decisions I've ever made.

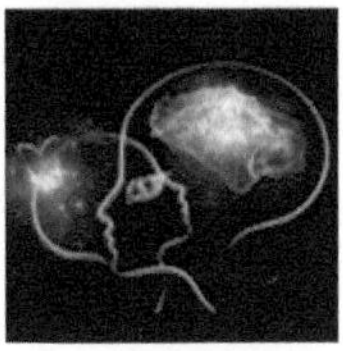

CHAPTER 3

IMPACT OF STRESS & TRAUMA ON MOMMY BRAINS

It was 10:00 AM, I waited outside Megha's house on my two-wheeler, eager to meet Aditi and hopefully find a way to ease some of the stress in my life. Megha guided me through narrow streets, barely wide enough for a single bike. The roads were dirty, littered with trash, and the air was filled with an unpleasant smell. I started second-guessing my decision to come and thought of returning. The area looked old, with cracks in every building, faded paint, and crumbling walls. The houses were packed so close together, and each one was incredibly narrow.

We parked the bike, blocking the road, and knocked on a door. A woman answered. Her hair was slightly messy, and her complexion was dark but she radiated life and energy. She was beautiful and glowing with bright, expressive eyes that held both strength and kindness. Her natural, warm smile was instantly welcoming. Her aura seemed to light up the space around her. I had never seen such vibrancy before. Megha introduced me to Aditi.

"Namaste," I said, surprised.

I had imagined Aditi to be in her 50s, but she looked more like she was in her twenties. She greeted us with a smile and let us inside. Two little kids were sitting on the floor in a small space where there was hardly room to move. A small cot rested against the wall, and on it sat an elderly woman. Megha introduced me to Aditi's children, Janani and Dhruv, and her mother.

I looked around the room. The entire house was just a small room with one bathroom—no separate kitchen, bedroom, or living room. Aditi invited me to sit on the cot next to her mother. I nodded as if I was okay standing—a decision I regretted later. Megha took the seat I was offered.

"Aren't we supposed to go out?" I asked.

"No, not yet," Megha replied, settling on the cot.

Aditi's mom looked irritated, clearly not happy with Megha for sitting on her cot.

"How are you, aunty?" Megha asked, trying to start a conversation.

Her mom didn't respond, and Megha didn't seem bothered. I felt a little out of place. But Megha kept talking to her. Frustrated, her mom shot me a look as if she'd hated me her whole life. I felt embarrassed.

Sensing my discomfort, Megha said, "This is Aruna aunty."

"Aunty, this is Prashanthi, my friend. She's a good friend. Say hi to her," Megha said.

I couldn't figure out what was going on. "Is something wrong with her?" I whispered to Megha.

"She has dementia," Megha explained.

Dementia is a condition that affects the brain, causing a decline in cognitive abilities. People with dementia often struggle with memory, clear thinking, problem-solving, or speaking. They often forget recent events, get confused about time or place, and their mood or behavior may change. Dementia is caused by various diseases, with Alzheimer's being the most common.

A few minutes later, Aditi appeared.
"I'm ready. Let's go," she said.

"Mom, take care of the kids," Aditi told her mother.
Confused, I asked, "She has dementia—how can she watch the kids?"

Aditi smiled. "Don't worry, the kids are used to her. Plus, my friend will be coming over too."

We walked to a nearby community hall. It was a small room in an old building, with a leaky roof, rough floors, and peeling paint. When we arrived, about 15 people were already waiting for Aditi. As soon as they saw Aditi, they rushed over, surrounding her so quickly that I lost sight of her. They spoke to her in a language I didn't understand. I just stood there, confused and watching.

Megha called out to Aditi. "We'll catch up with you later. Finish up here."

Aditi smiled and stayed with the group. Megha and I stepped outside, walking down the narrow streets that all looked the same. I worried I might get lost.

"What's going on? Who is Aditi? Why are they living here? And why were those people flocking to her?" I fired one question after another at Megha.

Megha sighed deeply, then looked at me. "I've known Aditi for a couple of years now. I heard about her from one of my clients. Aditi helped her through a really rough time. But it wasn't just her—Aditi has helped many others struggling with mental health issues."

I was confused. How could someone who is barely scraping by help others?

Before I could ask more questions, Megha interrupted, "If you really want to understand Aditi, you must know her story," Megha said, her voice softening as she began.

Aditi was a cheerful child, growing up in a small village with her brother Raghu. She spent her days running through the fields, trying to catch butterflies, always smiling and spreading happiness to those around her. But when Aditi turned eight, her life took a dramatic turn. The family had to move to a bigger city because of her father's business. Life in the village had been fulfilling. The open spaces and connection with nature made everything feel refreshing. But in the city, everything was cramped. They felt trapped in a concrete jungle. Aditi couldn't see butterflies anymore. It felt like the free-spirited girl inside her had been caged too.

Slowly, Aditi and Raghu adjusted to their new surroundings and made friends with the local kids. One day, while playing cricket, Raghu was hit on the head by a ball. Although there were no visible injuries, he suffered a brain hemorrhage, which led to his death. This tragedy shattered their family. Aditi's mother was in shock for days, and her father, struggling to care for his grieving family, was cheated by a business partner. Aditi had to drop out of school for two years. At a very young age, she took on the responsibility of caring for her mother, even though she, too, needed care. She shouldered responsibilities far beyond her years. Her father, unable to handle the pressure, gave up the business. With no income, the family struggled to make ends meet. Slowly, Aditi's mother, Aruna, recovered, but it took four long years before life started to feel somewhat normal again. Aditi's father, Deepak, started a new business and learned to invest in the stock market, eventually regaining financial stability. Aditi grew up, but the pain of losing Raghu remained. Her mother never seemed to bond with her the way she used to.

As Aditi entered her high school years, she faced bullying. Other kids body-shamed her, making fun of her looks. She often felt isolated, with no one to turn to. Despite these challenges, Aditi pushed through and earned a master's degree in bioinformatics, landing a job at a pharmaceutical company.

But in 2008, the stock market crashed, and her father lost everything. The loss was too much for him to bear, and he took his own life. This broke Aditi's mother even further. She was already living with the unbearable grief of losing her son, and now she had lost her husband too. While trying to survive at her new job, Aditi had to take on the responsibility of caring for her mother once again, managing the household finances, and supporting them both.

With all the pain Aditi carried, she had to set aside her dreams of marriage and a family. Her whole world became her mother and her job. As time passed, her mother began showing signs of depression and memory loss. Aditi was deeply concerned, but her mom had one final wish—to see her daughter married before it was too late. After years of bad luck following her, Aditi believed she would never find someone, until Vikranth came into her life.

Vikranth, an army officer, was visiting his hometown on vacation. During his stay, he went to see his friend Gaurav, who happened to be the owner of the pharma company where Aditi worked. It was there that Vikranth saw Aditi and immediately felt drawn to her. Despite her quiet nature and reserved demeanor, he saw something special in her—a quiet strength that captivated him.

When Gaurav noticed Vikranth's interest, he shared Aditi's story, telling him about her difficult past and the struggles she was still facing. Hearing about her hardships only made Vikranth admire her more. He approached Aditi and her mother, expressing his desire to marry her. Aditi was shocked that someone could be interested in her, especially after all the body-shaming and emotional trauma she had endured. But Vikranth was sincere—he told Aditi she could continue living with her mom and care for her. His kindness touched her heart, and soon after, they got married.

After a month, Vikranth returned to work, and Aditi remained with her mother. A few weeks later, she found out she was pregnant. But instead of joy, she was overwhelmed with anxiety. Old fears haunted her—what if her child died like her brother? What if her husband left like her father?

She was constantly worried, and the stress eventually caused her to miscarry. This heartbreaking pattern repeated itself two more times over the next three years. After losing three pregnancies—at four, seven, and nine months—Aditi was left physically and emotionally drained.

She developed a rare anxiety disorder and had to take time off from work, spending all her time caring for her mother, who had now begun to forget even Aditi's name. Desperate, Aditi sought medical help. After several doctor visits, she learned her mother was developing dementia—a condition that would worsen without proper care.

Aditi, determined to help her mother, dived into learning everything she could about dementia, brain damage, and how these changes affect a person's life. What Aditi didn't realize, however, was how much damage her own brain had suffered from the relentless trauma and stress she had endured. Though she appeared normal and healthy on the outside, her experiences had deeply shaped how she saw the world. She was now living with the long-term effects of unresolved pain and emotional turmoil. And Aditi's story is not the only one like this…

Almost every woman lives under the shadow of stress caused by various factors—physical, mental, emotional, social, and economic pressures. Issues like gender discrimination, unequal pay, lack of support systems, and uncertainty, especially during the childbearing years, all take a toll. Research indicates that maternal stress during pregnancy is associated with adverse outcomes, including preterm birth and low birth weight, often requiring additional medical interventions (Dunkel Schetter & Tanner, 2012).

These stresses lead to more frequent hospital visits and increased dependence on medications, making it harder to sustain a natural balance. The following are common side effects of stress and trauma new mothers face:

Consequences of Stress and Trauma for New Moms

- **Brain Changes:** Ongoing stress and trauma can shrink the hippocampus (memory) and over activate the amygdala (emotions), limiting the brain's adaptability (Lupien et al., 2009).
- **Depression and Anxiety:** High stress increases the risk of postpartum depression and anxiety, affecting bonding and daily tasks.
- **Post-Traumatic Stress Disorder (PTSD):** Traumatic experiences, including a difficult childbirth, can lead to PTSD, causing hypervigilance, avoidance, and intrusive thoughts. Recent studies have highlighted that postpartum PTSD can significantly affect a mother's ability to initiate and maintain breastfeeding, further complicating the postpartum experience (Ahsan et al. 2023).
- **Hormonal Imbalances:** Stress raises cortisol levels, disrupting mood and overall health.

- **Sleep Issues:** Stress leads to poor sleep, worsening fatigue and mental clarity.
- **Emotional Struggles:** Stress makes it harder to manage emotions and respond calmly to a baby's needs.
- **Isolation:** Trauma often leads to feeling isolated, preventing new moms from seeking support.
- **Relationship Strain:** High stress strains relationships, leading to conflict or a lack of support.
- **Cognitive Impact:** Stress affects memory, focus, and decision-making, making caregiving harder.
- **Reduced Adaptability:** Chronic stress limits the brain's ability to adapt, reducing positive postpartum changes.
- **Attachment issues:** Past trauma affects emotional availability, making it harder to bond with children.
- **Passing Down Trauma:** Research in epigenetics suggests that unresolved trauma can be transmitted across generations. Children of mothers who experience chronic stress or PTSD during pregnancy may have altered stress responses and an increased risk of anxiety disorders later in life (Yehuda & Bierer, 2009).

It's no surprise that women with high levels of stress are at a greater risk of autoimmune diseases such as heart disease, diabetes, Alzheimer's, arthritis, and even cancer. Research on early childhood adversity and toxic stress shows that prolonged exposure to stress hormones can have lifelong effects on physical and mental health (Shonkoff et al., 2012). From childhood, every experience leaves an imprint on the brain, shaping how we see the world and respond to challenges.

To reduce the risks of stress and trauma, it is crucial to prioritize brain health before the damage becomes chronic. As we age, the brain's ability to adapt and recover decreases, making it harder to bounce back. However, with strong willpower, determination, and a supportive environment, healing and improvement are possible—just like in Aditi's life.

In the next chapter, we'll explore how Aditi confronted and healed from her stress and trauma, rising stronger than before. We'll also dive into why brain care is often overlooked, the myths surrounding it for new moms, and what happens when mental barriers are lifted, unleashing the true potential of the mommy brain.

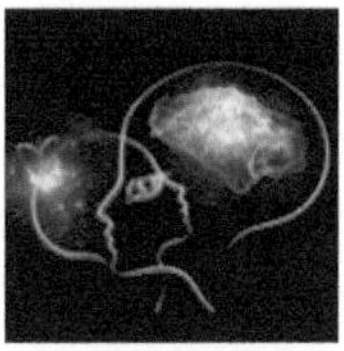

CHAPTER 4

WHY BRAIN CARE IS NEGLECTED

While many studies highlight the importance of brain health during pregnancy, most of this information doesn't reach families due to a lack of awareness. Various barriers prevent mothers from prioritizing their brain care.

Brain care is often overlooked in new moms for several reasons. After childbirth, the focus is mainly on physical recovery—such as healing from delivery and breastfeeding. This can overshadow the importance of mental health, leading to the belief that physical recovery is the only priority.

Nita experienced this firsthand. After her baby was born, everyone around her asked how her stitches were healing or how breastfeeding was going. No one asked how she was feeling emotionally. She brushed off her sleepless nights and moments of tearfulness, thinking they were just part of being a new mom. But deep down, she felt lost, overwhelmed, and disconnected.

Many people, including healthcare providers and new mothers, may not fully understand the brain changes and mental health challenges that come with motherhood. This lack of knowledge can lead to the neglect of brain care. There is also a stigma surrounding mental health issues, especially for new mothers. Admitting to struggles like postpartum depression is often seen as a weakness, making women hesitant to seek help.

In some cultures, there is an emphasis on self-sacrifice, where mothers prioritize their family's needs over their own. This can lead to the neglect of mental health and brain care. Postpartum care typically focuses on immediate physical needs, with little attention given to long-term mental health, leaving brain care unaddressed.

Caring for a newborn can be overwhelming, leaving little time for self-care. New mothers may prioritize their baby's needs over their own mental health. Many also face financial pressures and time constraints that make it difficult to focus on brain care.

Limited access to resources like therapy or support groups further contributes to this neglect. Without a strong support system, new mothers may struggle to find time and resources for their mental health. Isolation can increase stress and anxiety, making brain care even harder to prioritize.

Finally, many believe that motherhood should come naturally and that any struggles are a sign of failure. This mindset can prevent new mothers from seeking help for cognitive or emotional challenges.

Even when mothers want to improve their mental health, many myths about brain care stop them from focusing on it.

Here are some myths about brain care:

MYTHS ABOUT BRAIN CARE:

Myth: You Should Just Focus on the Baby, Not Your Own Mental Health
Reality: A mom's mental health is important for both her and her baby. Taking care of your brain and mental health helps you both.

Myth: You Need to "Tough It Out" Alone
Reality: New moms shouldn't face challenges alone. Getting help from family or friends is important and benefits mental health.

Myth: Postpartum Depression Only Affects the Weak
Reality: Postpartum depression can affect any new mom. It's caused by hormonal changes and requires proper care.

Myth: Brain Health Only Declines After Motherhood
Reality: Motherhood doesn't always harm brain health; in fact, it can improve certain skills. A 2016 study by Hoekzema et al., published in *Nature Neuroscience,* found that new moms experience growth in gray matter in areas of the brain linked to empathy, emotional regulation, and social understanding.

While "mommy brain" may make some feel forgetful, studies show that mothers become better at remembering baby-related information and managing emotions. The hormone oxytocin, which increases during pregnancy and breastfeeding, enhances bonding, stress resilience, and social skills (Marlin et al., 2015). These changes show how the brain adapts to make moms stronger and more capable over time.

Myth: It's Normal to Feel "Off" for Years After Birth
Reality: Some mood changes are normal, but feeling "off" for a long time may mean you need help. Brain health is important.

Myth: Supplements Alone Can Fix Brain Health Issues
Reality: Supplements can help, but they are not enough. Eating well, exercising, sleeping, and mental health care are all necessary.

Myth: If You're Not Happy All the Time, Something's Wrong
Reality: It's normal to have mixed feelings after becoming a mom. Expecting to be happy all the time can cause stress. It's okay to feel a range of emotions.

Myth: You'll Get Back to "Normal" After a Few Months
Reality: What feels "normal" changes after having a baby. The brain adapts to motherhood, and finding a new balance can take time.

Aditi also believed that brain care was not important or that it could be considered selfishness. However, Vikranth was deeply worried when he found out Aditi was pregnant again. Although he loved children, his concern for Aditi overshadowed the joy of becoming a father. He constantly feared—what if this pregnancy ended in another miscarriage? What if something happened to Aditi? He knew he had to do something. But every time he tried to help; Aditi turned him down. She didn't want counseling or therapy. This time, though, he was determined to help her return to a normal life.

Desperate, Vikranth decided to take her somewhere for a change of environment. He made arrangements for Aditi's mother to be taken care of, and they flew north, where Vikranth was stationed. As an army officer, he often traveled to different parts of the Himalayas and would take short breaks in the peaceful surroundings. He hoped the fresh air and beauty of the mountains would help Aditi feel a change and start to heal. Soon, they flew to Himachal Pradesh.

WHAT HAPPENS WHEN THE BRAIN IS TAKEN CARE OF

Growing up, Aditi had never traveled outside her village and the city she lived in. The fresh air immediately caught her attention, and the breathtaking beauty of nature overwhelmed her senses. She felt a new kind of energy flowing through her body. The moment she stepped into nature's lap; she felt a sense of care—something she longed for all her life.
For the first time in years, Aditi was reminded of the little 8-year-old girl she used to be—running barefoot through the fields, chasing butterflies without a care in the world. She remembered the joy of laughing freely, the warmth of the sun on her face, and the simple happiness of being in the moment, completely untouched by worries. But in the next instant, the weight of her past returned, and she realized how much trauma had buried that innocent part of her. The little girl who once chased butterflies had been trapped deep inside, locked away by years of pain. Within seconds, she was pulled back into her present struggles, and the tears began to flow.

Vikranth convinced Aditi to meet Pranav, a clinical psychologist and an old friend. Pranav specialized in cognitive-behavioral therapy (CBT) and had years of experience helping war survivors and others heal from deep emotional trauma. Vikranth was certain he could help Aditi too.

When Aditi met him, his calm and compassionate approach made her feel safe. But as she began sharing her struggles, she broke down in tears. Vikranth stepped in to explain everything Aditi had been through.

Pranav gently reassured her that she could not only live a normal life but also find true happiness again. His words sparked a small glimmer of hope in her eyes. He explained how our thoughts shape our minds and how, sometimes, they can hurt us more than the trauma itself. Intense emotions from painful experiences can trap us in the past, making us relive those moments over and over. In that moment, as Pranav spoke, Aditi felt a flicker of hope.

She began to understand—her mother was stuck in the memories of her brother's death, shutting herself off from the world around her. Pranav's words felt like a light breaking through the darkness.

Aditi listened as Pranav asked her about her fears of having children. She opened up about how her mother abandoned her after her brother died, leaving Aditi to shoulder the family responsibilities. She expressed her fear of losing or abandoning her own children, just like her mother had. The first day of treatment lasted two hours, and by the end, Aditi felt a heavy weight lift off her shoulders.

Over the next month, she learned how thoughts shape the brain and how meditation could help shift her perspective and rewire her brain. She also began meditating under Pranav's guidance. Within two months, she saw significant progress and learned how to apply these techniques in her daily life.

After returning home, Aditi poured her heart into practicing everything she had learned. During her mother's checkups, she paid close attention, absorbing every detail about how the brain works and how the mind shapes the body.

She also started reading books on brain function, searching for answers beyond what she had known before. Among them, one book stood out—*You Are the Placebo* by Dr. Joe Dispenza. A single line from the book changed everything for her:

"The moment you change your thoughts, you change your biology."

It struck her like a revelation. As a pharmacist, she had always known about the placebo effect—how, in drug trials, people sometimes felt better after taking a sugar pill simply because they *believed* it would work. But she had never truly considered what that meant beyond the lab. Now, she saw it in a different light. *Could belief alone influence healing? Could hope be just as powerful as medicine?*

The idea fascinated her. She realized that when combined with proper care and medical treatment, the mind's ability to influence the body could create profound changes. It wasn't about blind faith; it was about harnessing the brain's untapped potential to aid recovery.

Meeting Pranav and learning about brain function and meditation had already planted a seed of hope within her. Now, as she put these insights into practice, something within her shifted. The weight of anxiety that had gripped her for years began to loosen. She no longer felt like a prisoner of her past or her fears.

For the first time in a long time, Aditi allowed herself to believe that healing was possible.

As she saw her own progress, Aditi began to trust in the mind's power over the body. Within three years, she was blessed with two beautiful babies and experienced a profound inner transformation after becoming a mother. She had never been happier. Instead of doubting whether she would abandon her kids like her mother had, she developed hope. She realized she was no longer living in her past; she was creating her own future. As she nurtured positive feelings, her body healed, and her confidence grew. With this newfound strength, she felt a deep desire to help others who felt lost and hopeless, just as she once had.

However, Aditi's journey over those three years was not without difficulty. There were times when she mourned and felt hopeless. After becoming a mother, she experienced a new surge of energy—a fierce, protective force that awakened within her. Having faced trauma, she became more vigilant. Yet, with the positive reinforcement she had gained in the mountains, Aditi grew stronger and more confident. She became deeply aware of what was happening both within her and around her.

This awareness helped her overcome her fears and become the mother she had always wished to be.

By the time Megha finished telling me Aditi's story, it was already lunchtime. I was hungry and tired. Megha took me to see Aditi, who was still chatting with people, looking as fresh as she had that morning—without breaking a sweat. Meanwhile, I had just been sitting and listening to Megha, feeling starving, sweating, and smelling terrible. How did Aditi manage that? I also found out that Aditi wasn't in her twenties—she was in her forties. What was her secret to staying young and energetic despite everything she had been through? I wanted to be like Aditi. I admired her charisma and beauty. I realized she had faced much tougher challenges than I had, and if she could overcome them, then I could too. And I should.

After Aditi wrapped up her work, I approached her, feeling genuinely happy to meet her. I told her I was eager to join her work and learn from her. She asked me a little about myself, and I opened up, sharing everything—my education, my career, and the challenges I was currently facing. I explained how I had completed my post-graduation in Biotechnology but had somehow ended up working in a bank, which I eventually had to leave because of personal issues I was still struggling with. I admitted that I was in desperate need of help to manage my stress and anxiety.

Aditi listened intently before saying.

"Understanding the brain is key to tackling life's challenges." She explained that the brain isn't just an organ—it's the core of who we are.

"Since you studied biology, you've made my job easier," she said with a smile.

I didn't fully grasp what she meant, but I had a feeling she understood exactly what I needed.

Her words stayed with me, making me realize how little attention we give to our brains, even though they shape every part of our existence.

I began to wonder—how often do we really think about the brain itself?

So far, we've discussed why brain care is often overlooked, especially for new moms, and addressed some common myths that contribute to this neglect. We've also seen how prioritizing brain health can lead to profound changes in one's life.

Now, let's explore the fascinating world of the brain itself—how it functions, what it really does, and why it is at the core of everything we are. The more you understand your brain, the clearer it becomes: it's not just a part of you—*it is you.*

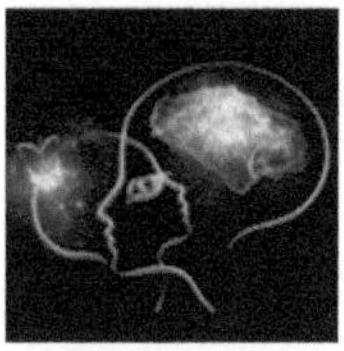

CHAPTER 5

KNOW YOUR BRAIN
(YOU ARE YOUR BRAIN)

"I am a brain, Watson. The rest of me is a mere appendix."
—Sir Arthur Conan Doyle

I kept thinking about what Aditi said. How can I overcome my fears? Should I, like her, go to the Himalayas? But even if I did, I would worry about the journey because of my fear of heights and the freezing cold. Doubts filled my mind.

A week later, Aditi called. "We're going to the Brain Museum in Bangalore," she said.

I hesitated but agreed, unsure why she had chosen this place. Another week passed, and we set off for the NIMHANS Brain Museum—the only brain museum in India.

The moment I stepped inside, a strong smell filled the air—formaldehyde, the chemical used to preserve organs. Rows of human brains, some whole, some partial, lay behind glass cases. Many showed signs of damage, silent witnesses to lives once lived. Yet, as I stood there, it felt as if these brains were speaking to me—not in a haunting way, but in a way that carried deep meaning.

Each brain told a story: a stroke that stole speech, a disease that erased memory, an injury that reshaped personality. These weren't just specimens—they were windows into the human experience.

The brain isn't just an organ tucked in the skull; it's a meaning-maker, floating in cerebrospinal fluid, gathering, interpreting, and weaving information. It blends memory and experience, emotion and action, shaping our biology.

But beyond its biology, the brain is a storyteller. It constructs our reality, crafting the world we see, hear, and feel. It filters every experience through the lens of our past, giving meaning to our emotions and shaping the way we respond to life.

Is it possible that everything we experience is just a crafted story?

Our brain seems filled with **"magical logics"** and **"logical magics"**—a perfect blend of science and wonder. I couldn't help but fall in love with this three-pound wizard (brain) instantly. It wasn't just controlling my life—it was creating it, moment by moment.

I thought back to Aditi's words. "You made my job easy."

At first, I assumed she was speaking to the science student in me. But as I stood there, staring at the preserved brains, I realized she had awakened something else—the artist in me. The brain wasn't just a biological marvel—it was a masterpiece, a living work of art shaping reality itself.

In that moment, I felt an overwhelming sense of awe.

As I gazed at the preserved brains, I couldn't stop thinking: How did this all begin? How did a simple cluster of cells evolve into this complex organ capable of thought, memory, and emotion?

"The brain's journey is one of nature's greatest stories, spanning billions of years of evolution," Aditi explained.

With her unique way of storytelling, she began spoon-feeding complex science into my mind, making it surprisingly easy to grasp.

The brain wasn't always this complex. Its journey began billions of years ago, as life itself took shape.

THE STORY OF THE BRAIN

A long time ago, life evolved from single cells to more complex structures. These single cells grouped together, each taking on specific roles—some handled digestion and protection, while others focused on reproduction. This division of labor helped living things survive and reproduce.

Over billions of years, our bodies learned to automate these essential functions, with the nervous system acting as the command center. It connects the brain to the body through the spinal cord and a vast network of nerves, constantly sending signals to coordinate movement, reflexes, and vital functions.

If you step on something sharp, you instinctively pull your leg back. If you touch a hot pan, your hand jerks away before you even realize it. This rapid communication helps you respond instantly, protecting you from harm. But the nervous system does more than just react—it defines the very boundaries of your body.

From head to toe, the nervous system senses everything that comes near. A mother's touch? Safe. A thorn pressing into the skin? Dangerous. But how does it know the difference? This ability to distinguish between safety and danger led to the evolution of the brain—the most complex organ of all. It didn't just react to the world; it learned from it, remembered it, and adapted.

But the nervous system doesn't just protect us from physical harm—it also shields us from emotional and psychological threats.

When we face serious emotional or physical danger—like encountering a tiger or even our boss who feels like one—the nervous system activates a strong response called **"fight, flight, or freeze."** In this survival mode, the brain releases hormones like adrenaline to prepare the body for action and cortisol to maintain energy during stress. These hormones send blood to our arms and legs, so we can either confront the threat, escape, or freeze in place.

Once the danger is gone, our body slowly returns to its **"rest and digest"** mode, allowing normal functions to resume. During this time, the brain releases hormones like serotonin and melatonin, helping us relax and recover.

This fight or flight response has helped humans survive for millions of years—but it doesn't just prepare us for life-threatening situations. One of the most intense times a human experience this response is during childbirth.

During labor, a mother's body is flooded with stress hormones. A study by Alehagen et al. (2001) found that adrenaline and cortisol levels spike by more than **500%**, while noradrenaline levels rise by about **50%**. This extreme spike pushes the body into survival mode, keeping the mother highly alert. However, if she remains in this heightened state too long, it can slow recovery, disrupt emotional balance, and weaken the immune system. Sleep disturbances, weight gain, and an increased risk of heart disease can also follow.

Notably, more than one-third of women experience lasting health problems after childbirth—highlighting the critical need for comprehensive postnatal care (WHO, 2023).

Childbirth is not just a physical event—it is a deeply neurological one. The brain plays a key role in how a mother responds to stress, adapts to change, and recovers after birth. Understanding how the brain works can help new moms navigate these challenges with greater awareness and ease.

To understand the brain, you don't need a laboratory or a microscope. Just watch your baby. No one understands the brain better than a mother.

THE BRAIN

Look at your little one. Can they do anything on their own? Can they solve a problem? No. They are simply breathing, cooing, and crying—basic survival instincts. All they know is that when they cry, mommy comes to feed, comfort, and protect them.

Why? Because their brain is still growing.

Now, think back to your own childhood. You were born the same way—helpless, dependent, and slowly learning how to navigate the world. Unlike many animals that can walk and survive on their own shortly after birth, human babies take years to develop. And this has been happening since humans first evolved, nearly two million years ago.

This isn't a flaw; it's nature's design. When our ancestors started walking on two legs, their bodies changed. Their hips became narrower, making childbirth more difficult. If babies were born with fully developed brains, their heads would be too large to pass through the birth canal.

In other words, delivering a fully developed newborn brain would make childbirth impossible—neither the mother nor the baby wouldn't survive (Dunsworth et al., 2012).

So, nature chose survival. Babies are born early, their brains still unfinished, designed to grow outside the womb, shaped by the world around them *(David Eagleman, The Brain: The Story of You).*

But here's the part many mothers overlook: just as a baby's brain grows and adapts, so does a mother's brain.

Motherhood is like becoming a child once again—thrown into a world of unknowns. With hormones fluctuating, a baby demanding constant attention, family expectations, and societal pressures to "do it all," you can feel lost and helpless.

Before you even realize what's happening, you are carrying the enormous responsibility of raising another helpless being who needs you every moment.

With your brain rewiring itself for motherhood while simultaneously managing stress, exhaustion, and emotions, the pressure can feel overwhelming. It's like falling from the top floor all the way to the ground floor.

THE THREE BRAINS

To understand this better, let's first explore the three levels of the brain (MacLean, 1990):

1. Lower Brain (Reptilian Brain/Ground floor): Controls basic functions like breathing, heartbeat, and survival instincts.
2. Middle Brain (Emotional Brain/Middle floor): Manages emotions and memories, shaping how we respond to the world.
3. Upper Brain (Frontal Cortex/Top floor): Responsible for logic, reasoning, and problem-solving—what makes us human.

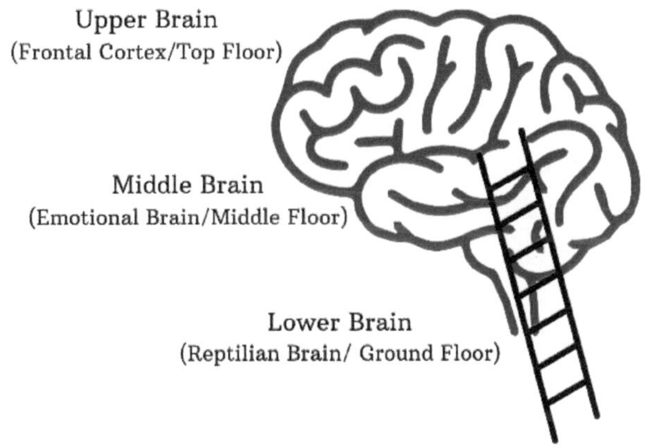

The frontal cortex is the brain's front region, responsible for higher thinking like reasoning and problem-solving. Within it, the prefrontal cortex—located just behind your forehead—acts as the control center, helping with planning and decision-making.

When the frontal cortex doesn't develop properly, a person may physically grow but struggle with reasoning, impulse control, and emotional regulation. Think of Kiran from Chapter 1. Though her body grew, her brain remained at the level of a one-year-old due to her early brain injury.

Newborns rely mostly on the lower and middle brains. They respond emotionally rather than logically because their prefrontal cortex—the part that helps with thinking and decision-making—is still developing. Over time, as they experience the world, their brain grows stronger, improving their ability to think, solve problems, and regulate emotions.

This is why brain health is critical—not just for newborns, but also for new moms. A mother struggling with her own brain health may find it harder to regulate emotions, remain present, or make rational decisions.

If you think the brain is just the organ that sits in our skull, you're very wrong. There's another brain, deep within our gut, that plays an equally important role in our mental and emotional well-being.

As new mothers, we are bombarded with advertisements promoting DHA-rich foods, fortified formulas, and brain-boosting supplements for infants. This is because brain health is deeply connected to nutrition—not just for babies, but for mothers too.

This brings us to an important question: How does food shape the brain? And what role does gut health play in brain function?

THE SECOND BRAIN

Have you ever noticed why you can't think straight when you're hungry or why you crave unhealthy foods even when you know they're bad for you? Or perhaps you've felt those butterflies in your stomach during a stressful moment? That's because your gut and brain are in constant conversation.

The gut has its own network of neurons—so many that it's often called the "Second Brain" or the enteric nervous system (Cryan et al., 2019). At the heart of this connection is the vagus nerve, which carries messages between the gut and the brain.

But the real power inside your gut isn't just nerves—it's the trillions of microorganisms living there. Your gut is home to tiny living bacteria called microbiota. The number of these bacterial cells is almost equal to the number of your own human cells, but their genetic material is far more diverse. While we carry about 20,000 to 25,000 human genes, the gut microbiota holds over 3 million genes, about 150 times more than human genome (Qin et al., 2010). This means they have an enormous influence on your biology. These tiny helpers quietly support digestion, strengthen your immunity, and even shape your mood and emotional well-being.

In *The Mind-Gut Connection,* author Emeran Mayer explains that gut bacteria don't just aid digestion; they actively influence our emotions, stress levels, and even decision-making. He describes how signals from the gut travel to the brain, shaping our moods and behaviors in ways we don't even realize. These microbes communicate with the brain through the gut-brain axis, producing hormones like serotonin, which regulate mood and cognition.

However, gut bacteria are highly sensitive. Stress, poor diet, lack of sleep, and even a single night of sleep deprivation can disrupt their balance (Benedict et al., 2012). Research shows that just a few hours of stress can damage gut bacteria, and it takes time for them to recover (Bailey & Coe, 1999). This explains why stress can lead to stomach issues and why the food we eat can influence our brain function.

So next time you choose what to eat, think about these tiny creatures in your gut that depend on your diet. Sometimes, food that feels good at the moment can actually harm them. Gut imbalances can be caused by many factors, including alcohol, smoking, antibiotics, poor diet (too much sugar, processed foods, unhealthy fats), obesity, dehydration, a sedentary lifestyle, chronic stress, hormonal changes.

If these problems aren't addressed, they can lead to chronic gut issues like irritable bowel syndrome, digestive disorders, diabetes, and autoimmune diseases (Belkaid & Hand, 2014).

While pregnancy cravings can be hard to resist, returning to a regular diet is essential for restoring gut bacteria. Since many of us eat emotionally rather than logically, it's crucial to be mindful of how we feel about food.

Just as our gut influences our brain, another vital part of our body affects our brain and shapes our emotions—the heart. The heart is where life begins and ends, holding our core emotions and feelings in its secret chambers.

THE LITTLE BRAIN

Think back to that first scan after you got pregnant. Around 21 days, you saw that tiny flicker on the screen—the heartbeat—that confirmed new life. Although you can't hear it yet, the soft "lub-dub" brings immense joy and excitement. This tiny heart, the very first organ to form from those early cells, is more powerful than we can imagine. It's not just a pump; it's the place where our deepest feelings—love, joy, trust, anger, and sadness—are born. With every beat, the heart sends signals to our brain, shaping our emotions and connecting us to life in profound ways.

In 1991, Dr. J. Andrew Armour discovered that the heart has its own "Little Brain." This "heart brain" contains about 40,000 neurons, similar to those in the brain. It can learn, remember, and feel on its own. The heart sends more signals to the brain than it receives, influencing decisions and emotions.

Researchers have found that the heart sends powerful messages to the brain—not only does the brain listen, but it also obeys. The heart plays a leading role in shaping our thoughts and feelings. In fact, its electromagnetic field is the strongest in the body, even influencing those around us.

The HeartMath Institute found that emotions directly affect heart rhythms. For example, during the 2008 stock market crash, more people experienced heart attacks likely due to stress and anxiety. This shows how closely our emotional state impacts heart health (McCraty, 2015).

Negative emotions can disrupt the heart's rhythm, causing stress and leading to issues like blocked arteries. This emotional burden can have lasting health impacts. For example, some people may die shortly after losing a loved one, due to the strong emotional connection between partners (O'Connor et al., 2023).

For a long time, I believed the heart was merely a pump that circulates blood. But through my pregnancy and Aditi's guidance and insight, I came to realize it is so much more. It's not just a "little brain"; it's the "boss brain," shaping our reality and deeply influencing our emotions and experiences.

Though the second brain and little brain influence our brain health, there's another hidden player behind the scenes, running the show on autopilot: "the subconscious brain."

THE SUBCONSCIOUS BRAIN

Every morning, your mind races with countless thoughts—about work, finances, or what to wear today. You might think about buying a house or a car, or whether it's time to relocate. You may even worry about which daycare is safest for your child. But have you ever noticed how your body keeps functioning without effort? Your heart beats, your lungs breathe, and your food digests—all without your conscious involvement, even when you are lost in your worries or sound asleep.

When was the last time you paid attention to these automatic processes? How does your body know to keep everything running smoothly? The answer lies in your "subconscious brain"—the silent force working behind the scenes, controlling 95% of your daily life (Lipton, 2005).

Now think about your baby. Remember how much effort they put into learning to walk or talk? Every step was a struggle. But when was the last time you had to consciously think about walking or speaking? These actions are second nature now—because once a skill is mastered, the subconscious takes over.

In *The Biology of Belief* (2005), Bruce Lipton states, *"The subconscious mind is a million times more powerful than the conscious mind"*. It's not just a storage unit for past experiences—it's the hidden programmer shaping our behaviors, habits, and emotional responses. Once something is learned, the subconscious takes over, freeing the conscious mind to focus on new things. It doesn't just help you survive—it determines whether you thrive.

Daniel Kahneman, in *Thinking, Fast and Slow,* describes how our brain operates using two systems—System 1, the fast, automatic, subconscious mind, and System 2, the slow, logical, conscious mind (Kahneman, 2011). System 1—the subconscious—makes most of our decisions before our conscious mind even catches up. This explains why certain habits, fears, and emotional triggers feel deeply ingrained.

Since childhood, our subconscious has recorded everything—how we walk, talk, eat, and even what we fear. These patterns, etched deeper than ancient carvings, dictate our daily choices. They act as a master alchemist, releasing hormones and chemicals that shape our reality through habits and emotions.

And this is where the real challenge lies. We may set conscious goals—to eat healthier, exercise, or build confidence—but our subconscious follows the patterns it has always known. Grabbing a glass of water is simple, but making a change in a habit—even a small one—can feel like climbing a mountain. Think of how many times we start a diet and give up within a week, or join a gym but stop going after a month. The subconscious mind resists change.

In *The Power of Your Subconscious Mind,* Joseph Murphy explains, *"What you impress upon your subconscious mind will be expressed in your reality"* (Murphy, 1963). The subconscious doesn't distinguish between positive or negative—it simply follows whatever patterns have been most repeated. If we constantly tell ourselves, "I'm not good enough" or "I always fail," our subconscious ensures those beliefs play out in our lives.

This means that many of the beliefs we hold today—about ourselves, success, or even our fears—were programmed long before we were aware of them. As Vishen Lakhiani explains in *The Code of the Extraordinary Mind* (2016), we often live by *'Brules'*—unquestioned beliefs passed down by society, family, or culture—without realizing how they shape our subconscious and limit our potential.

I spent much of my childhood trapped in fear—shaped by taboos, superstitions, and deep-seated beliefs. I once panicked for days after accidentally eating an omelet on a "forbidden" day. I had been taught that breaking this rule would bring misfortune or something bad would happen.

Even after years of education, subconscious fears still haunted me—extending beyond superstition into gender inequality, stereotypes, racism, and economic disparity.

With a deep sigh of hopelessness, I believed there was nothing I could do about it.

As I walked through the museum, surrounded by silent remnants of lives once lived, I couldn't stop wondering—how had their subconscious minds shaped their choices, their fears, their destinies?

But that day, as I held a human brain in my hands, everything changed. It felt heavier than I expected—not just with cells and neurons, but with the essence of a person's existence.

***

The brain wasn't just a piece of organic mass; it was a masterpiece, holding the imprint of an entire life within its neural networks. Each connection told a story—some like fairy tales, and some like scary tales. The brain literally grew out of experiences and memories, evolving with every challenge and triumph.

I turned to Aditi, my voice barely above a whisper. "It's incredible." I felt both in awe and strangely overwhelmed.

Holding the brain in my hands, I added, "I feel so privileged to hold such a profound symbol of life—something that once carried a person's entire existence."

As I was about to place it back, Aditi stopped me.

"You're not just privileged to hold a brain from the past," she said, her voice steady.

"You have the privilege to shape the brain of the future."
I looked at her, puzzled.

Taking the brain from my hands, she continued, "Your subconscious mind was shaped long before you had any control over it. But right now, your child's subconscious is forming—through you. If you see the world through a lens of fear and insecurity, your child may adopt the same view. And sometimes, it can take a lifetime to unlearn."

Her words hit me like a wave. I suddenly realized how my daughter absorbs everything around her—what she sees, hears, and feels. Her brain is like a sponge, soaking up not just words and actions but also subtle, unspoken cues—body language, gestures, and even deeply held beliefs.

She follows me even when I'm not walking. She listens to me even when I'm not talking.

This trust is both empowering and terrifying.

What if I unknowingly misled her? What if she inherited my fears and insecurities instead of growing into her full potential? What if my own beliefs held her back rather than helping her flourish?
A deep sense of shame settled over me. The weight of responsibility pressed down on my shoulders.

"What if I'm already shaping her future in the wrong way?"

The thought was overwhelming, even frightening.
Aditi met my gaze, her expression calm yet firm. She gently placed the brain back on the table, paused, then said,

"In the earliest years of life, a child's mind is wide open, absorbing everything—words, emotions, even silent fears. During this time, the brain is incredibly receptive (Lipton, 2005), making it easy for beliefs and behaviors to take root. Siegel and Bryson (2012) explain that the brain's capacity to absorb and store information during these formative years lays the foundation for the child's emotional and cognitive development. This period is crucial for shaping the way a child perceives the world and interacts with it.

That's why it's often said, 'Give me a child for the first seven years, and I will show you the man.' If a child repeatedly hears, 'You're not good enough' or 'Money is hard to earn,' those messages don't just disappear. They settle deep, shaping how they see themselves and the world, often without them even realizing it."

"By the time we turn seven, much of who we are has already been shaped—our character, habits, emotional responses, and even the way we see the world. Since babies share an unspoken bond with their mothers, they don't just absorb words; they take in the emotions, fears, and subconscious patterns their mothers carry."

I swallowed, hard.

Aditi exhaled; her voice softer now. "I carried so many subconscious fears," she admitted. For years, I carried childhood traumas, believing that my life was a waste. Those buried fears didn't just haunt me—they manifested in my body, leading to multiple miscarriages."

"I work with so many mothers every day who struggle with the same thing," she continued. They fear that their insecurities will seep into their children's lives. And honestly, that fear is well-founded.

My chest tightened. I wasn't alone in this.

I looked at her, taking in every word.

"You may not be able to completely change your subconscious overnight," she continued, "but you can train your brain to make conscious choices that benefit you.

"It's never too late," she said. "If you want to live a fulfilling life, both for yourself and your daughter, you need to start taking care of your brain right away."

"It takes effort, time, and patience. Sometimes you'll slip back into old habits. But to embrace new ways of thinking, you have to unlearn outdated patterns. Just like planting new seeds requires preparing the soil, you must cultivate your mind to make it fertile again. This might bring back childhood doubts and fears, but don't let that stop you from living the life you dream of."

Aditi's words stirred something in me—a mixture of fear and hope.

Aditi had become a powerful example of transformation. At that moment, I knew I had a choice. I could stay trapped in my subconscious doubts and fears, or I could take the first step toward change.

I don't have all the answers yet, but for the first time, I felt ready to embrace change.

In the next chapter, I'll share how just 'three minutes' completely changed my life—and why heart-brain coherence became a game changer. We'll also explore how meditation helped me to see the impossible—what was always within me, quietly waiting to be noticed: the hidden power of 'mommy brain.'

Before diving into the next chapter, let's briefly recap what we've learned so far.

Quick Summary:

1. Brain's Role: The brain is a powerful organ that processes emotions, thoughts, and actions, shaping our reality.

2. Brain Evolution: From survival instincts to advanced reasoning, the brain connects the mind and body.

3. Stress Response: The brain activates survival mechanisms during danger but needs balance to prevent harm, especially for new moms.

4. Three Brains:

    - Lower Brain: Survival.
    - Middle Brain: Emotions.
    - Upper Brain: Logic.

5. Gut-Brain Connection: A healthy gut supports brain health and mood.

6. Heart's Influence: The heart's "brain" affects emotions and connects deeply.

7. Subconscious Mind: Past experiences shape 95% of our actions and habits.

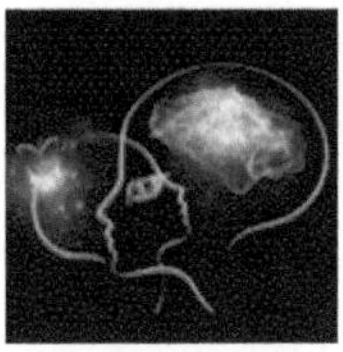

CHAPTER 6

THE UNKNOWN POWER OF THE MOMMY BRAIN

With all the motivation Aditi gave me, I felt inspired and began following her lead. I committed to rewiring my subconscious mind and adopted every healthy habit I could find. I focused on consuming nutritious foods and worked on pushing away the negative thoughts that once consumed me.

Aditi encouraged me to meditate and observe my breathing. Since it was difficult to visit her place daily, she suggested I meditate at home whenever possible. However, I was skeptical about the results. Still, with nothing to lose, I agreed to give it a try. After all, I thought, it wasn't rocket science—it should be easy, just a matter of observing my breath.

Just like we make New Year's resolutions, I made a resolution to regulate my mind through meditation. The next day, I woke up early, sat on my couch, closed my eyes and began. I thought an hour had passed, but when I opened my eyes, I realized I had only been sitting for a few seconds. I tried again, this time setting an alarm for five minutes so I wouldn't open my eyes until it went off.

Those five minutes felt like the longest of my life. A million thoughts rushed through my mind, and I thought rocket science would have been easier than silencing all these thoughts. Time stretched endlessly, and I eventually got so tired that I fell asleep. My resolution to use meditation for brain regulation suddenly felt like too much work.

I pushed through for a week, but after that, I started avoiding it. I told myself I was too busy, that I didn't have time for meditation. What I didn't realize then was that my "Muggle Brain" was scared of the silence. My subconscious mind, resisting change, was working against me, preventing this new habit from sticking. I continued living my fear-filled life, not giving much thought to meditation.

After leaving my job, I felt like I had lost a part of my identity. In my fear of losing myself, I struggled to bond with my baby. To fill the void and connect, I showered her with toys and material things, turning myself into a "Material Mom." But she would only play with them for a while before tossing them aside, as if all my effort to provide meant nothing to her.

Meanwhile, the "Banker Brain" in me focused on balancing our finances and easing the weight of our growing bills, trying to lift some of the burden off my husband's shoulders. Eventually, I found a new way to relax—*trading*.

I dusted off my demat account and began binge-trading and investing. It was exhilarating, giving me a high greater than that of a casino. But the fear of losses made me more volatile than the market itself.

I kept myself busy with various activities, believing I was doing my best for my daughter's future. But in the process, I pushed my research aside—it was going nowhere.

Just as I thought everything was getting under control, fate threw me into a situation that reminded me just how fragile life can be.

The Three Minutes

I joined swimming classes with my daughter. One day, during class, I was swimming from wall to wall when something went wrong. In the middle of the pool, I started choking and panicking. The fear of drowning kicked in, and I was fighting for my life.

The seconds dragged on, stretching into what felt like an eternity. Somehow, I managed to cry out for help. A professional rescue person threw me a buoyancy ring, and I clung to it tightly as they pulled me out of the water. The whole ordeal lasted less than three minutes.

But that three-minute struggle was just the beginning. Over the next three months, I faced a series of health issues—swimmer's ear, sinus infections, dizziness, headaches, sleep apnea, and more.

While antibiotics helped with the infections, their frequent use caused side effects, leaving me more vulnerable to other illnesses. My body grew weaker. I felt emotionally unstable, plagued by brain fog, restless sleep, and low energy.

And it didn't stop with me. My husband and daughter caught my illnesses, dragging our entire family into an exhausting cycle of hospital visits and treatments that lasted for over a year. Each setback chipped away at my strength, leaving me more vulnerable than ever.

As my health continued to decline, I remembered Aditi's words about the power of breathing and meditation. Back then, it had seemed unnecessary—just another thing to add to an already overwhelming to-do list. But now, my body and mind screamed for an uninterrupted breath.

Feeling utterly helpless, I turned to Aditi. She was my only hope.

Desperate, I called her and poured out everything. She listened in silence. Then, in a calm but firm voice, she urged me to meet her in person.

Without hesitation, I agreed. I needed immediate help.

A War within

When I finally met Aditi, it felt like stepping into an emergency room—just like the time years ago when I faced a physical crisis.

But this time, the emergency wasn't visible. It wasn't a broken bone or a fever. It was deeper, harder to define, and even harder to heal.

The moment I saw her, the weight of my struggles overwhelmed me. Tears streamed down my face as I broke down, confessing how I had neglected the most fundamental part of life—the very thing I desperately needed at that moment.

"Breathing."

Aditi held space for my emotions, her calm presence grounding me. When my sobs subsided, she spoke—her voice steady, yet carrying a calm firmness that made every word resonate deeply. Her words still echo in my mind:

"Now you understand the true difference between survival stress—real life-or-death situations like the one you faced in the pool—and pseudo-stress, which is what most of us experience today. Peer pressure, stock market crashes, 24/7 breaking news, an unflattering picture on social media, a troll… none of these are life-threatening, yet our bodies react as if they are."

She paused, letting the words settle.

"Our brains are wired this way. Our ancestors faced real dangers—wild animals, famine, the daily struggle for survival. Back then, stress meant life or death. But today, we live in urban jungles that didn't even exist in the hunter-gatherer era. And yet, our minds still react to modern stressors as if we're being chased by a tiger."

Her words hit me like a bolt of truth.

"Think about how hard it must have been for them to survive—to protect future generations so we could live better lives. And yet here we are, still trapped in the primitive fears of survival instincts."

"We no longer fight for survival, yet modern stress is killing us in a different way. Anxiety, depression, and chronic illnesses are rising. Diabetes, heart disease, obesity, cancer—these aren't just medical conditions; they're the result of chronic stress. We are more connected than ever through technology, yet loneliness is at an all-time high. We're more comfortable than ever, yet we're running on invisible hamster wheels, unsure what we're truly working for."

"We've built incredible things—skyscrapers that touch the clouds—but we've forgotten to build up our own mental resilience. The strength to weather life's storms. We've connected the world, but we've forgotten how to connect with ourselves. If we don't learn to take care of our minds, future generations will face the same existential threat."

She took a deep breath, her words hanging in the air.

"And that is why mothers must become strong and resilient. Because the stronger the mother, the more resilient the child."

A heavy silence filled the room.

Her truth shattered me. I needed a moment to process everything she had said. Slowly, I nodded. Deep down, I had always known she was right. But hearing it laid out so clearly made it impossible to ignore.

She had just described my life. The battles I fought every day—chasing distractions, balancing finances—weren't life-threatening, yet they had consumed my mind as if they were. I had let stress control me, and my body was paying the price.

Gathering my courage, I finally asked the question that had been burning inside me.

"What's the solution?"

Aditi studied me for a long moment before responding.

"You already know the answer."

I shook my head, "I don't."

She exhaled deeply, then spoke a single word:

"Meditate."

Her voice softened as she added, *"Meditation is the medication for most of life's struggles."*

She let that sink in before continuing.

"Meditation brings your heart and brain into harmony, creating a balanced state called **'Heart-Brain Coherence.'**

To help me understand, she shared an insightful study about how heart-brain coherence not only transforms personal well-being but also impacts entire societies.

The Heart's Hidden Connection

In 2015, a group of scientists set out to investigate a deep question: Could human heart rhythms actually sync with the Earth's magnetic field?

To find out, they studied 104 people from different parts of the world—California, Lithuania, Saudi Arabia, New Zealand, and England. Each participant wore a small device that tracked their heartbeats for 15 days, while specialized instruments measured the Earth's shifting magnetic fields in their locations.

The results were astonishing. On March 5th, the participants practiced a 15-minute meditation called *Heart Lock-In (HLI)*, focusing on deep, slow breathing and positive emotions like love, gratitude, and peace. During this short practice, something remarkable happened—their heart rhythms became smoother, more balanced, and, incredibly, aligned with the Earth's magnetic fluctuations.

The study revealed that when people experienced positive emotions, their heart and brain worked in harmony—a state known as **"heart-brain coherence."** But stress and negativity could disrupt this balance, creating erratic heart rhythms that make communication between the brain and heart more difficult.

Even more fascinating, the research showed that not only did individuals sync with the Earth's magnetic field, but their heart rhythms also became more synchronized with each other. It was as if their hearts were "talking" to one another in a silent, rhythmic language. *(McCarty et al., 2015, Global Advances in Health and Medicine).*

***

With Aditi's encouragement and the hope, she gave through the study, I started meditating again—to bring some light to my darkness-filled life.

Every time I was distracted, I remembered those three minutes when I struggled in the swimming pool, gasping for air, fighting the fear of drowning. And *the importance of breathing.*

To bring in coherence, I explored various breathing techniques—from the ancient wisdom of yogis to modern science. Pranayama, box breathing, and more. Each one has its own power. I also practiced different forms of meditation—the Silva Method, Vipassana, and others. Each offered unique benefits.

Slowly, I could meditate without feeling drained. But I had no idea what this simple practice would lead to.

The Hidden Power of Mommy Brain

One day, during a family trip to the beach, I was struck by the beauty of nature. Sitting by the shore, I could hear the waves, feel the fresh breeze, and watch the ocean dance in perfect rhythm.

I took a deep breath, letting the salty air fill my lungs, and then something shifted inside me. Within moments, my heartbeat synced with the ocean's rise and fall.

In that stillness, I wasn't just sitting by the ocean—I felt like I was part of it. The same force that pulled the tides was moving through me. I could feel it—the invisible energy that sustains all life. Some call it *"Life Force Energy."* Others call it *"Prana"* or *"Chi."* Whatever its name, it was the same force that moves the tides, sways the trees, and keeps the planets in motion.

I closed my eyes, letting the thought settle in. All my life, I had taken breathing for granted. But now I understood—breathing isn't just survival. It's life itself. It's the first thing we do when we enter this world and the last thing before we leave. Everything in between? Just borrowed time, measured in inhales and exhales.

Yet how often do we forget to truly breathe?

As new moms, we give so much of ourselves away—our time, our energy, our very essence—pouring into our endless responsibilities. We hold our breath through sleepless nights, tantrums, and silent worries. We carry invisible weights—self-doubt, exhaustion, the pressure to be the perfect mother—until we're drained, running on empty.

But in doing so, we forget a simple truth—breath isn't just something we take; it's something that gives back to us. It nourishes. It sustains. It restores.

Breath is the bridge between the seen and unseen, between the chaos of daily life and the calm we long for.

I inhaled deeply, feeling the energy move through me, and for the first time in a long while, I felt truly alive.

And all it took was a deep breath.

With each inhale, I felt the life force energy flowing through me—through my organs, tissues, cells, down to the very molecules that made up my body. And in that stillness, I saw the undeniable truth—this same energy had once created life within me. From two microscopic cells—a sperm and an egg, a whole new being had formed, grown in perfect harmony with the universe.

Sitting by the ocean that day, I understood something profound. Just as I once carried my baby in my womb, I, too, was being carried—by something vast, something unseen. A force that had never let me go, even when I felt lost.

For the first time, I understood the true purpose of the "Mommy Brain." It's not just about nurturing and protecting—it's about transferring life force energy through me to my baby, helping her connect with Mother Nature, and being a part of the universe's bigger plan.

A deep, soul-soothing calm washed over me—a quiet knowing that I was being held, cared for. A gentle presence surrounded me—not seen, but deeply felt. It was as if invisible hands were resting on my shoulders.

A whisper echoing through my heart: *"It's okay."*

"It's okay to be imperfect. It's okay to worry. It's okay to feel lost. *You are held. You are cared for. You are never alone."*

At that moment, I didn't just understand it—*I knew it.*

Had this force always been there, waiting for me to notice?

Was this what pure, unconditional love felt like—embracing me in its *cosmic womb*?

As calmness settled in, a wave of love swept over me—not just for my baby, but for life itself.

Tears welled in my eyes.

My problems hadn't disappeared. My finances were still tight. My responsibilities hadn't changed. Yet, something within me had shifted. The world around me—once chaotic and overwhelming—now felt strangely peaceful. As if, for the first time, I could breathe without the weight of worry pressing down on me.

But as soon as I opened my eyes, the invisible force pulled me back into the hamster wheel of life. The endless to-do list. The silent pressures. The unspoken fears.

And that's when it hit me.

I wasn't running from real dangers. I was running from the tigers in my mind.

Not from the predators in the wild, but from the fears I had carried for too long—the fear of losing myself, of falling behind, of not being enough. My brain, wired for survival, had kept me in a constant state of alertness. Always running. Never resting.

And then, another truth struck me.

The battle wasn't outside me—it was within me.

A war between two versions of myself. The **conditioned** brain—shaped by years of expectations, responsibilities, and struggles—fighting against the **mommy brain**, the part of me that was raw, unfiltered, and deeply connected to life itself.

At the heart of this war were **two powerful forces—the Mother Molecules and the Other Molecules.**

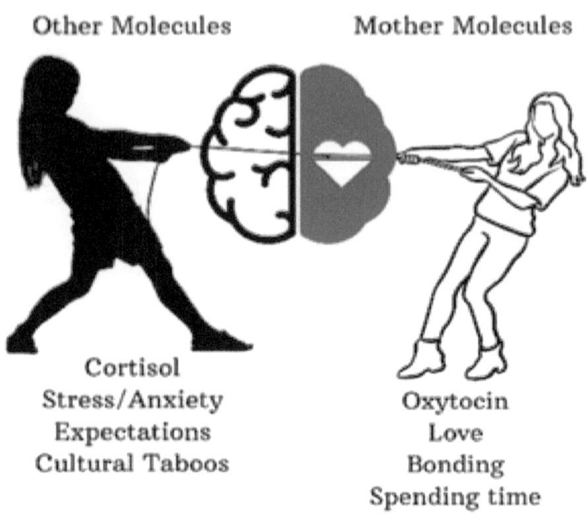

The **Mother Molecules—**the very hormones that made me a mother—oxytocin, prolactin, the surges of dopamine that filled me with love for my baby—were constantly at war with the **Other Molecules—**the spikes of cortisol, adrenaline, and the relentless forces—pushing me to 'bounce back.' The constant stress, financial worries, societal pressures, the longing to reclaim my old self. Cortisol battled oxytocin. The need to provide clashed with the need to rest. The longing to be "me" wrestled with the desire to be fully present with my child.

And in this exhausting war, I wasn't physically tired—I was emotionally drained.

But as I took a deep breath by the ocean, something softened inside me again.

I felt held. Not by anything external, but by life itself.

This reality shift brought myriad questions that stirred my heart.

How can a simple pause bring such a profound shift? Is it the power of stillness? The beauty of silence? Or is it that in nothingness, everything exists?

I sank into deep thought, absorbing the vibrant colors of the ocean, not knowing that those very colors held the answers I was searching for.

***

So far, we've explored how my life changed in just three minutes, how I discovered the power of breath, the magic of heart-brain coherence, and the hidden power of the mommy brain.

In the next chapter, I'll share my struggle to baby-proof my brain, the unexpected wisdom from an ancient African tribe, and the colorful lesson that reshaped my reality.

We'll also explore how these experiences transformed me—how they helped me step into a new version of myself, stronger, more resilient and more grounded than ever before.

And most importantly, we'll uncover why a **holistic** approach to life isn't just a choice—it's a necessity.

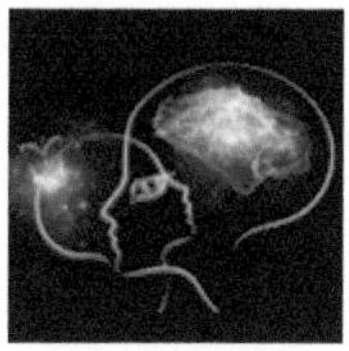

CHAPTER 7

BABY-PROOF YOUR BRAIN

When a baby arrives, we baby-proof our home—covering sharp edges, locking cabinets, and making sure everything is safe. But there's one place we often forget to baby-proof—the most important home we live in: ***our brain.***

Motherhood rewires our brains, and if we're not careful, stress, self-doubt, and overwhelm can sneak in like sharp edges left uncovered.

But here's something interesting—our brains thrive on challenges. They adapt, reshape, and grow stronger with the right stimulation. It's like the saying, *"What doesn't kill you makes you stronger."*

Except for me, even after experiencing deep peace near the ocean, I couldn't silence my mind. That moment of calm should have lasted, but instead, it awakened even bigger questions about life, purpose, and meaning.

My thoughts, once limited to my own struggles, began to expand—pulling me into a silent war within.

The Silent War

My mind felt caught between two worlds. On one side were the philosophies I had embraced—ideas of mindfulness, trust, and surrender. On the other, the harsh realities of life—bills to pay, responsibilities to meet, and an uncertain future.

How could I hold on to bliss when the weight of bills pulled me back to reality?

I tried everything to quiet my racing mind—meditation, exercise, dancing, even singing my heart out. They helped, but the silence never lasted.

And then, one day, something unexpected happened.

I found an unexpected trick to silence my mind—coloring and crafting with my child.

At first, it was just another activity to keep her engaged. But as I mixed colors and cut out shapes, something inside me softened. The swirls of paint, the way colors blended into each other—it reminded me of the ocean.

The same ocean that had once given me a deep, soothing assurance.

And that's when I truly understood.

Colors are magical.

They don't just fill the world around us—they shape the world inside us.

The Colorful World

Colors tell stories. They evoke different emotions. But my understanding of color changed completely when I stumbled upon a documentary about an ancient African tribe—the Himba tribe of Namibia.

The Himba people don't have a specific word for blue. To them, blue blends with green. And because of this, they struggle to see blue at all.

Researchers showed them a circle of green squares with one blue square hidden among them. To an outsider, the blue stood out instantly. But to the Himba, it blended right in—they couldn't see the difference.

Yet when shown different shades of green—shades that looked identical to outsiders—they could instantly spot the tiniest variations (Roberson et al., 2000).

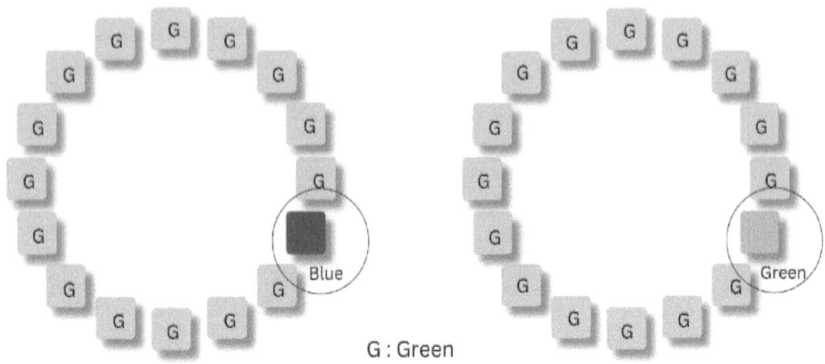

It was mind-blowing.

If an entire tribe can struggle to see a color simply because they lack a word for it, then what am I blind to—just because I lack the words or awareness to describe it?

This realization made me question: **If we can be blind to colors, can we also be blind to our own emotions?**

For years, I labeled my racing thoughts as anxiety, my exhaustion as weakness.

But what if it wasn't anxiety at all?

What if it was **unresolved grief**?

What if my stress wasn't a flaw, but a sign my brain was adapting to a new reality?

Just like the Himba couldn't see blue, had I been blind to parts of my own experience simply because I had never been given a language to describe them?

This idea of perception shaping reality reminded me of something more recent—an Internet debate that left the world divided.

Remember The Dress?

Some people swore it was blue and black, while others saw white and gold.

The same image, two entirely different realities

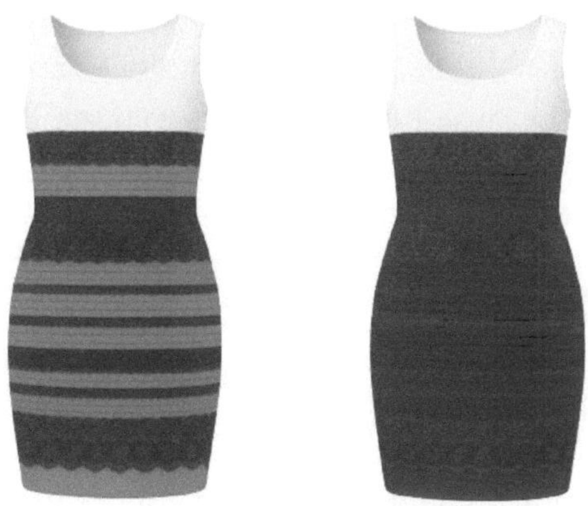

'*The Dress*' phenomenon revealed how our brains interpret color based on context, with lighting cues influencing whether we see white and gold or blue and black (Gegenfurtner et al., 2015).

The truth is, the colors don't exist in the way we think. Light reflects off objects, and our eyes pick up certain wavelengths. Our brain then translates those signals into color.

Color is created inside our heads.

***

A Shift in Perspective: A Mental Drift

If colors—something that seems so absolute—are shaped by our perception, then what about our experiences?

What if just like the Himba tribe, I wasn't experiencing true reality, simply because I had no words to describe them?

Am I experiencing the true reality, or just the story I tell myself?"

If my brain could create colors that didn't exist, then what else was it shaping?

If pain is absolute, wouldn't we all experience it the same way? Then why do struggles feel heavier for some and lighter for others?

Could it be that our interpretation—not the event itself—determines our suffering?

What if my limitations, my struggles—were just illusions I had the power to rewrite?

That idea amazed me.

Since then, I began rewriting my inner script—choosing a more positive narrative for every experience, even my deepest struggles.

Instead of asking, *"Why is this happening to me?"* I started asking, *"What is this situation teaching me? How is this making me stronger?"*

Instead of drowning in guilt or self-blame, I looked for the lesson. Instead of focusing on problems, I started searching for solutions.

And I never imagined where this simple practice would lead me.

THE TRANSFORMATION BEGINS

Little did I know that this newfound perspective would soon reveal itself in the simplest of moments—while crafting with my daughter.

One day, as I was making a cardboard house for her, I mixed paints, watching colors melt into each other, forming new shades.

Curious, she asked, *"Mommy, how are you making so many colors?"*

I smiled and said, *"It's magic, dear."*

But the real magic happened inside me.

The Gestalt Shift in Motherhood: Seeing the whole

In the early days of motherhood, I felt like I was losing pieces of myself. My sharp, independent mind felt foggy. My old dreams seemed distant. I called it "Mommy Brain," but in my heart, it felt more like "Losing Myself Brain."

But that day, as I watched two colors blending into a new shade, something clicked.

Motherhood had done the same to me.

I wasn't losing myself—I was transforming.

My muggle brain (my regular brain) and my mommy brain weren't fighting for space. They were blending to create a new shade of me—merging into something richer, wiser—something entirely new.

This is where the Gestalt perspective changed how I saw myself.

Gestalt psychology teaches us that the whole is greater than the sum of its parts. It's not just about the individual pieces—it's about how they come together to form something bigger, something meaningful.

When I looked at my life in fragments, I felt broken. But when I stepped back and saw the bigger picture, I realized I wasn't falling apart—I was becoming whole.

I wasn't lost; I was evolving.

Motherhood isn't just sleepless nights, endless responsibilities, and moments of self-doubt. It's also tiny hands reaching for yours, a baby's laughter, the warmth of love so deep it reshapes you.

Yes, there were fears. The anxiety of being enough. The exhaustion of doing it all. The silent guilt of wanting time for myself—my identity.

But these weren't separate struggles—they were part of my growth.

Just like different shades of paint mix to create a new color, my experiences—both joyful and painful—were blending into a fuller, stronger version of me.

An upgraded and transformed version—a "Holistic Brain."

The Holistic Brain

The Holistic Brain taught me that life isn't about avoiding struggles—it's about embracing both joy and pain as equal parts of growth. Because when life gets tough—and it will—we don't crumble.

I realized true peace doesn't come from controlling outcomes—it comes from nurturing our inner world.

A holistic brain brings clarity, emotional strength, and resilience. It rewires old patterns, creating space for growth and transformation.

And when you nourish your brain, it nurtures you in return—helping you embrace life with clarity, peace, and energy.

It helps you shift your perspective and give deeper meaning to every experience.

From "Why is this happening to me?" to "What can I create from this?"

From "I have no control." to "I can choose how I see and respond to this moment."

The Holistic Path: The Only Way to Baby-Proof Our Brain

This transformation wasn't just a mental shift—it was a lifestyle change. Practicing a holistic lifestyle is the only way to truly baby-proof our brain.

Because no amount of external safety measures can shield a child from a mother drowning in anxiety, self-doubt, and exhaustion.

Living the "Holistic Path" means recognizing the power of creation—whether it's giving birth, writing a poem, composing music, or simply creating balance within ourselves.

Because the greatest creation of all is not just a life well-lived—**it's a life fully felt.**

To baby-proof our brain, we must strengthen its foundation. Just as a sturdy home stand on solid pillars, a holistic brain is supported by four essential ones.

The Four Pillars of a Holistic Brain

A holistic brain is built on four essential pillars: health, wealth, relationships, and integrity. Each pillar supports a different aspect of who you are, and together, they create balance and wholeness—helping you feel grounded and ready for each day.

Health: Physical, Mental, and Emotional

A holistic brain values health in all its forms—because mental exhaustion can block your brain just as much as physical illness.

My friend Riya, though physically healthy, struggled with anxiety and worry, which eventually led to depression.

This highlights that true health is holistic—it's not just the body, but the mind and heart too.

Wealth: Financial, Educational, and Emotional

True wealth isn't just money—it's feeling financially secure, continuing to grow, and nurturing emotional abundance.

Tripti, for example, once lived luxuriously, but after her baby's arrival, she became more conscious of financial security. More than money, she realized wealth also meant knowledge—learning about baby care empowered her.

And above all, wealth is happiness—cherishing small moments, like watching her baby sleep peacefully.

Relationships: Family, Social, Work, and Self

Relationships are at the core of a holistic life, and a holistic brain deeply values connections. This involves nurturing your bond with your partner, family, and friends.

At the same time, it's important to regularly check in with yourself, as the relationship you have with yourself lays the foundation for all others.

Integrity: Authenticity, Honesty, Transparency, and Humanity

Integrity is showing up as your true self—embracing struggles, asking for help, and honoring your needs.

A holistic brain means authenticity. Living with integrity not only empowers you but also sets a positive example for your child, teaching them valuable lessons about honesty and self-respect.

The Foundation: Spirituality

While these four pillars keep us balanced, they need a solid foundation—one that holds everything together when life shakes us.

That foundation is ***Spirituality***.

Spirituality isn't about following a strict doctrine or adhering to a belief system. It's deeply personal. It's about finding rituals that uplift your spirit and energize your soul.

Spirituality can be as simple as watching the sunrise, gazing at your baby, or feeling connected to the miracle of life itself.

Spirituality unlocks your inner potential, making you a magnet for life's true abundance—happiness, peace, love, and fulfillment.

When you see life through a spiritual lens, you stop merely surviving—you start thriving.

Creating a New Reality

Motherhood once felt like an endless series of tasks. But as I embraced this path, I began to see it as a shared journey.

My child wasn't just learning from me—I, too, was learning from her.

In her raw emotions and unfiltered curiosity, I saw a reflection of my own inner child—imperfect, curious, and always growing.

This transformation not only reshaped my life but also planted the seeds for a brighter future—for both me and my child.

I wish I had learned this sooner, but it's never too late to start.

And for the first time, I understood:

A well-nurtured brain is the greatest gift a mother can give her child because it shapes the way they see the world, think, and interact with others.

The strongest baby-proofing doesn't happen in our homes—it happens in our minds, and it starts with us.

As I began to reshape my reality as a mother, I realized this journey was more than just personal transformation—it was a career of growth and self-realization.

Mother: A New Holistic Career

Motherhood is not just a phase—it is a calling, a transformation, and a career in its own right.

A career that demands the sharpness of a leader, the patience of a teacher, the intuition of a healer, and the heart of a creator.

And when embraced holistically, it becomes not only one of the most powerful and fulfilling careers—but also the most empowering journey of self-realization.

Walking this path taught me that motherhood isn't just about what we do—it's about how we grow, think, and evolve along the way.

This Holistic Path didn't just teach me how to face my fears—it also taught me how to see abundance in my life. It wasn't about external success, but about training my mind to thrive.

Because success isn't material wealth—it's living in harmony with the gifts we are born with: our brains, our bodies, and our connection to life itself. It's about evolving with life's changes. It's about seeing beauty in all its forms.

***

So far, we've explored the importance of baby-proofing our brains—the struggles, the reality of the brain, the shifting perceptions, and how a holistic path transformed my life.

Now, it's time to take those insights a step further.

In the chapters ahead, I'll share practical, actionable steps to care for your brain.

Brain care isn't just about navigating motherhood with ease—it's about dancing with its flow, in grace and alignment.

And this… this is just the beginning.

When you begin to understand the true power of your brain, you don't just become a mother—you become an empowered being.

People start noticing something different in you. You've changed. You're glowing.

You become a magnet for happiness, joy, and peace.

You start living holistically.

Without even trying, you begin to influence those around you.

They start quietly watching, wondering, "How did she do it?"

But to reach that space, you must train your brain and body with the full presence of your soul.

And that's exactly what the coming chapters are going to offer: a guide to help you rise, a path to embody your true self.

Let's begin.

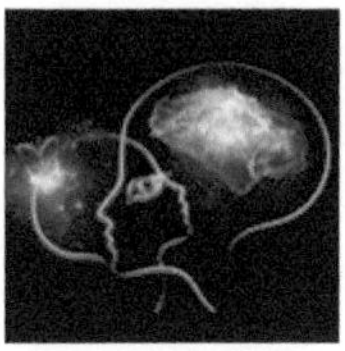

CHAPTER 8

BRAIN CARE FOR BUSY MOMS

TIME AND ENERGY MANAGEMENT

Motherhood reshapes time. Each day of pregnancy feels precious, but once your baby arrives, time seems to shrink—never enough, no matter how hard you try.

Your schedule is packed, your energy is stretched thin, and your emotions run high. Between feeding, diaper changes, and endless to-do lists, there's barely any space left for you.

Brain care? It doesn't even make it onto the list.

But here's the truth: taking care of your brain isn't a luxury—it's a necessity. When you prioritize your brain health, you're not wasting time; you're actually making time.

TIME: A Mother's Secret Currency

A well-nourished brain helps you think clearly, stay focused, and handle challenges with more ease. This allows you to get things done faster and have more time for what truly matters.

By prioritizing brain care, you're not just managing time; you're expanding it. A clear, energized brain helps you do more in less time.

However, even in the middle of chaos, your brain follows a natural rhythm. Understanding these brain rhythms can help you manage time and energy more effectively.

Understand Brain Waves

Your brain doesn't work at the same speed all day. It moves through different rhythms, called "brain waves," which influence your thoughts, emotions, and energy levels.

Have you ever noticed that some tasks feel easier at certain times? Or that your energy dips in the afternoon? That's because your brain operates in different states throughout the day.

Here's how they work:

- **Beta Waves (Busy Mode):** Your "go-go-go" mode—active when you're thinking, problem-solving, or multitasking. As a mom, you spend most of your day here! But too much beta activity can leave you feeling overwhelmed and exhausted.

• **Alpha Waves (Calm Mode):** Linked to relaxation and light focus. They show up during peaceful moments, like cuddling your baby or enjoying a quiet moment. Deep breathing can help shift you into this state.

• **Theta Waves (Recharge Mode):** Occur during light sleep and deep meditation, boosting creativity and problem-solving. A quick nap or a few moments of mindfulness can help you tap into this restorative state.

• **Delta Waves (Deep Rest Mode):** The slowest brain waves, active during deep sleep. This is when your brain heals, processes memories, and resets for the next day.

• **Gamma Waves (Peak Performance Mode):** The highest-frequency waves, linked to sharp thinking, fast decision-making, and deep concentration. They help you stay mentally alert, whether you're calming a fussy baby or handling a high-pressure situation.

BRAIN WAVES

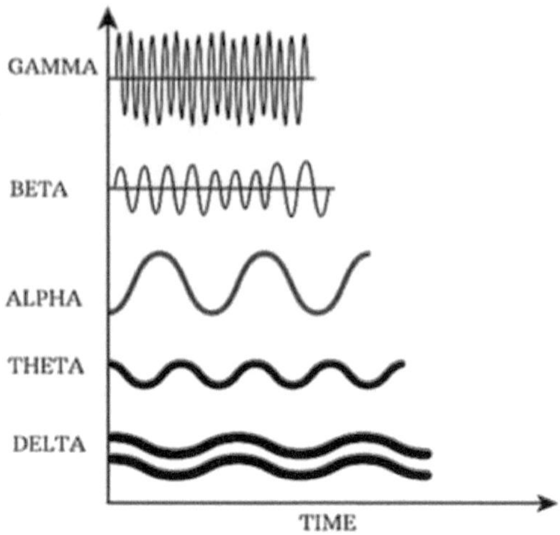

How to use this:

Pay attention to when you're stuck in Beta Overdrive—the high-stress state where everything feels overwhelming. When you notice this happening:

1. Pause.

2. Take a deep breath, count to three, and exhale slowly.

3. Repeat once more to further relax your mind.

By recognizing your brain's natural rhythms, you can shift gears as needed—leaning into focus when necessary and allowing yourself to recharge when possible.

Understanding brain waves gives you insight into your natural energy cycles.

Let's now explore how to make the most of those moments of focus and rest.

Get the Most Out of Less Time

For moms, time is gold—precious and limited. A distracted moment can feel like sand slipping through your fingers, leaving you frazzled. But even a few focused minutes can work wonders, offering a sense of control and accomplishment.

1. Time Pockets: Your Hidden Treasures

These are short, unplanned breaks scattered throughout your day—small moments that recharge you. Think of them as a funny scene in a serious movie—just enough to lighten the mood and keep you going.

Instead of letting these moments slip by unnoticed, use them to:

• Crack a joke or laugh at something silly.

• Do a quick, goofy dance with your baby.

• Stretch, close your eyes, or take a deep breath for a mental reset.

2. Mindful Moments

Never underestimate the power of pausing. Even tiny breaks can have a big impact. Savor a sip of tea, feel the warmth of the sun on your skin, or soak in your baby's smile. These little moments refill your emotional cup and bring you back to the present.

Quick Time-Saving Tips

1. **Brain Dump:** Write down your thoughts, worries, and to-dos. Clearing mental clutter helps you focus on what truly matters.

2. **Micro-Goals:** Break big tasks into tiny steps. Even completing one small step feels rewarding and keeps you motivated.

3. **The 5-Minute Rule:** If a task takes five minutes or less, do it immediately. These small wins add up to a productive day.

Just like a goldsmith carefully collects every scrap of gold, treat your time with care. When you manage it wisely, even the busiest days feel more balanced.

ENERGY MANAGEMENT FOR BRAIN HEALTH

Time management is only half the battle. If your energy is drained, even extra time won't help.

Your brain is like a marathon runner. Even though it makes up only 2% of your body weight, it consumes 25% of your body's energy—equivalent to running a marathon every single day. This means that even when you're just sitting and thinking, your brain is burning through fuel.

Have you ever felt exhausted after a tense phone call, even though you weren't physically moving? That's because mental strain drains your energy just as much as physical exertion.

Budget Your Energy, Not Just Your Time

Think of your energy like money in a bank account—limited but precious. Every thought, emotion, or task either spends or replenishes that energy.

- If you save an hour by skipping a chore but spend it overthinking or stressing, that time is wasted.
- If you use that hour to rest, recharge, or do something joyful, it becomes an investment in your well-being.

Ask Yourself:

- What energizes me? A walk in nature? A chat with a supportive friend?

- What drains my energy? A negative thought? Overthinking?

Managing energy means spending it wisely—just like managing finances. And to do this well, you must understand how emotions impact your energy.

The Link Between Emotions and Energy

Emotions are **"energy in motion"**—they can either fuel you or deplete you.

For example, planning your baby's birthday might start as exciting, but if self-doubt and stress creep in, the joy can turn into exhaustion.

In her book *Molecules of Emotion*, Candace B. Pert, Ph.D., explains that the same chemicals helping our brain and body work are also deeply tied to our emotions. These emotional messengers don't stay in the brain—they flow through the entire body, even reaching the immune system, showing how deeply the mind and body are connected.

Riding through the Ocean of Emotions

Unmanaged emotions can leave you feeling drained. But when you learn to understand and work with them, they can actually give you strength. This is where emotional balance becomes really important.

Think of your emotions like an ocean, and you're the one steering the ship.

When you have a healthy relationship with yourself, your ship stays steady. But if that relationship is shaky, it can turn into a battleship, leaving you lost and overwhelmed, caught in the storm.

The good news? You can learn to guide your emotions. With a few simple tools, you can stay calm and in control—even when the waves of life get tough.

Energy First Aid Kit: Tools for Emotional Management

When emotions overwhelm you, these tools can help you regain balance:

1. Dr. David Hawkins' Scale of Consciousness:

Dr. David Hawkins, a psychiatrist and spiritual teacher, created the Scale of Consciousness to measure emotional energy levels—from lower emotions like shame and guilt to higher emotions like love and peace.

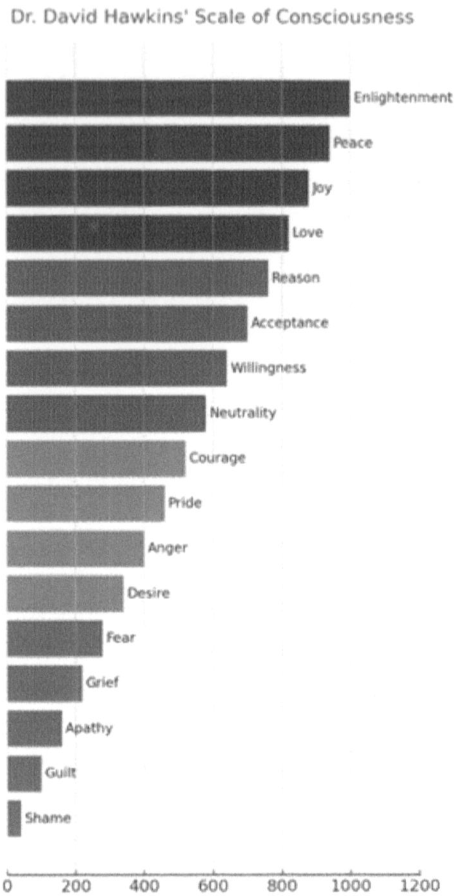

Understanding this scale helps you shift your mindset and elevate your emotional state.

Instead of thinking, "I can't do this," try: "I'm learning and growing through this."

This simple shift can boost your energy and resilience.

2. BOAT Method: Navigating Emotional Waves

When overwhelmed, use the BOAT method:

- Breathe: Pause and take deep breaths.
- Observe: Notice your emotions without judgment.
- Aware: Recognize tangled emotions (e.g., anger masking fear).
- Tag: Label the root emotion to regain control.

3. Ride the Waves

Emotions come and go. Instead of resisting them, let them flow. Trust that they will pass, and you'll emerge stronger.

4. Anchor Yourself

When emotions overwhelm you, grounding techniques can help you stay steady. Try simple methods like touching something solid, keeping your feet on the ground, or engaging all the five senses to stay anchored.

Quick Summary for Busy Moms:

- Your brain waves shift throughout the day. Learn to recognize when it's time to slow down.
- Prioritize tasks, batch them, and embrace small mindful moments.
- Treat your time and energy like gold—invest in what fills you up, not what drains you.
- Manage emotions by acknowledging them and finding ways to rise above negativity.
- Ride the waves of motherhood with resilience and grace.
- Recognize when your brain is out of energy, take time to refuel it.

Even if you can't apply all these tips at once, start with just one small shift. Progress, not perfection, is the goal.

Having explored how to manage time and energy for optimal brain health, take a moment to reflect on where you are in your own brain care journey.

Before we move on to the next chapter, use this small worksheet to assess and refine your approach.

Brain Care Worksheet

Mastering Time, Energy, and Emotions

This worksheet is designed to help you balance your brain waves, manage your time and energy effectively, and navigate emotions with mindfulness.

1. Brain Wave Tracking

Instructions: Reflect on your activities throughout the day. Identify the brain wave states you experienced and note supportive action taken—or needed—to optimize them.

Brain Wave State	What You Were Doing	Supportive Actions Taken (or Needed)
Beta (Focused Mode)	E.g., multitasking, planning	Took breaks, practiced deep breathing.
Alpha (Calm Mode)	E.g., relaxing after baby's nap	Spent quiet moments, listened to soothing music
Theta (Creative Mode)	E.g., daydreaming while feeding	Meditated, Visualized solutions, or rested
Delta (Rest/ Recovery Mode)	E.g., sleeping or dozing lightly	Reduced screen time, prioritized better sleep routines

Reflection: Which brain wave state do you need more of?

Now that you've reflected on your brain wave patterns, let's explore how to make the most of the small, hidden moments in your day for mindfulness or self-care.

2. Time Pockets for Mindfulness

Instructions: Identify small, often overlooked moments in your day—like during feeding, baby's nap, or while waiting—that can be used for mindfulness or self-care.

Time Pocket Activity	Mindful Action or Self-Care Idea
Feeding your baby	Focus on your breath, visualize calmness.
Baby's nap	Take a short nap, meditate, or stretch.
While cooking or cleaning	Practice gratitude, listen to calming music
Waiting during appointments	Reflect on emotions or practice BOAT.

Reflection: How can you maximize these small pockets to replenish your energy?

3. Energy Management

Identify Your Energy Levels

Instructions: Track your energy levels throughout the day on a scale of 1 to 5 (1 = very low, 5 = very high). Note what boosted or drained your energy.

Time of the Day	Energy level (1-5)	What were you doing?	What boosted or drained you?
Morning			
Afternoon			
Evening			
Night			

Reflection: What activities boost or drain your energy most? Which task was most fulfilling today, and how did it impact your energy?

How to Budget Energy

Instructions: Use the table to prioritize your tasks based on their importance and the energy required.

Task	Energy needed (High/ Medium/Low)	Can this be delegated or postponed

Smart Energy Management:

• **Tackle Important Tasks First:** Use peak energy for essential or creative work.

• **Balance Work and Rest:** Alternate between action and recovery.

• **Delegate Wisely:** Share tasks to conserve energy for what truly matters.

Reflection: How will you adjust your energy spending tomorrow?

4. Navigating the Ocean of Emotions

Using Dr. David Hawkins' Scale of Consciousness

Instructions: Identify your emotional state, its energy impact and actions to elevate your emotions.

Emotions Felt	**Energy Impact (Drain/Boost)**	**Action to Shift Higher**
Guilt, Shame, or Fear	Drain	Practice self-compassion or mindfulness
Anger or Pride	Mixed	Take deep breaths, find constructive outlets.
Courage, Acceptance, or Love	Boost	Acknowledge these emotions, and nurture them.

Using the BOAT Technique

BOAT helps you manage emotions with mindfulness and clarity.

Step	Your Reflection
Breathe	How did slowing your breath calm you?
Observe	What did you notice in your body and thoughts?
Aware	What emotions surfaced?
Tag Your Emotions	How would you label these emotions?

Reflection: How did BOAT help you row through the day's emotional waves?

How to Use This Worksheet

- Fill it out daily or weekly to track your brain wave patterns, time management, and emotional shifts.
- Reflect regularly to make small adjustments and celebrate progress.

Remember: Your brain energy deserves care, just like everything else in your life. Small steps make a big difference! You've taken the first step in understanding and nurturing your brain needs.

In the next chapter, we'll explore practical, science-backed tips to help recharge your brain so you can work smarter, not harder.

These simple yet powerful strategies are designed to boost your "mommy brain," keep your energy flowing, and help you thrive—not just survive—through the beautiful challenges of motherhood.

Let's dive in and discover these effective brain boosters!

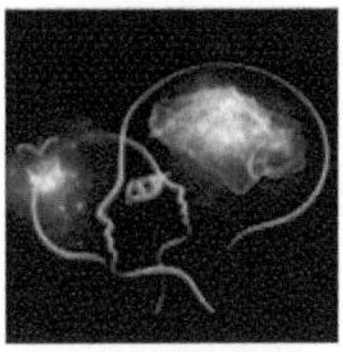

CHAPTER 9

RECHARGE YOUR MOMMY BRAIN

As we've explored throughout this book, your incredible 3-pound wizard—the brain—uses nearly 25% of your body's energy every single day. It never stops working. Even while you sleep, it's sorting, healing, and resetting itself. That's why it's so important to take good care of it.

But caring for an organ that doesn't feel anything isn't as hard as it sounds. Yes, you heard that right—the brain doesn't feel pain.

Have you ever heard that during brain surgery, some patients stay wide awake?

Yes, really.

It sounds impossible—but it's true.

The brain itself can't feel pain. It has no pain receptors.

So, surgeons don't use anesthesia on the brain—only on the scalp and skull. Once those layers are opened, the brain is touched directly… while the person is still conscious.

Imagine this:

A patient lies on the table. The room is silent except for the soft beeping of monitors. The surgeon gently touches a tiny spot on the exposed brain.

Suddenly, the patient's finger twitches.

Or a memory flashes before their eyes.

Sometimes, a foot moves.

Or they speak a sentence they didn't mean to say.

No one touched their body.

Only the brain.

And yet—it responded.

That's how powerful your brain is. It's not just sitting quietly in your skull. It's sending tiny electrical signals to every part of your body—controlling your breath, heartbeat, movement, emotions… even how you feel as a mother.

And here's the most beautiful part—the brain itself doesn't see, hear, or feel anything directly. It only knows what your eyes see, what your ears hear, what your body feels—and what your inner voice says.

So, how do you take care of this powerful organ—especially now, as a new mom?

Not by touching it.

But by changing what it experiences.

Your brain responds to everything around you. The voices you hear. The light in your room. The hugs you receive. The stories you tell yourself when you're alone.

And just like a surgeon uses gentle stimulation to activate certain brain areas, you can also "light up" your brain with simple, powerful habits.

Let's explore a few gentle hacks that support the brain inside your head:

Everyday Brain Boosters for Moms:

1. Feed it well: Your brain loves good food. Omega-3s from walnuts, flaxseeds, or fish are like brain fuel. Hydration helps too—water keeps your brain clear and your blood flowing.

2. Tell it better stories: Human brain feeds on stories. Deepak Chopra—a doctor, philosopher, and bestselling author, once said in an interview with Tom Bilyeu that his mother filled his childhood with fairy tales. Those stories shaped how he saw the world.

Your brain, too, grows stronger with kind, imaginative, or inspiring words—whether you're reading to your baby or speaking to yourself.

3. Create a calming space: Soft music. A cozy corner. The smell of lavender. These small things tell your brain: "You're safe." And when your brain feels safe, it can rest and heal.

4. Surround it with love: Hugs. Eye contact. Gentle touch. They all boost feel-good chemicals like oxytocin.

Candace B. Pert, a renowned neuroscientist and author of *The Molecules of Emotion*, once shared that during her intense research days, she would spend her breaks hugging her husband. She wasn't just being affectionate—she knew those hugs were helping her body release calming, healing chemicals like endorphins.

So don't underestimate a simple hug. Snuggle your baby. Hold someone's hand. Sit quietly with someone who feels like home.

Your brain senses that safety—even in silence.

Your brain may be hidden inside your head, but it's always listening.

To your breath. To your emotions. To the people around you.

So, give it something kind to listen to. Feed it gentle words. Surround it with warmth. You don't need expensive tools to care for your mommy brain.

You just need simple, loving habits—repeated every day.

But that's not all.

There's another brain quietly working below your belly—the second brain in your gut.

It listens, responds, and influences your mood, energy, and even your mommy instincts.

And it matters just as much.

Take Care of Your Second Brain: Your Gut Health Matters:

As we discussed in earlier chapters, your gut—also known as your second brain—is just as important as the one inside your head.

The saying goes, we are what we eat. But it's not just about eating healthy.

It's about how the food you eat turns into information. That information travels through your bloodstream—affecting how you feel, think, and behave.

Have you ever noticed how your mood lifts after a piece of chocolate or a sip of coffee? Or how sugar can suddenly give you energy—and then crash you down?

That's your gut talking to your brain. The food you eat directly impacts the chemicals released inside your body—like serotonin, dopamine, and even stress hormones.

So, when you feed your body, you're also feeding your mood, your energy, your sleep—and even the quality of your breast milk.

You're not just eating for yourself. You're eating for two nervous systems—yours and your baby's.

A healthy gut also supports a strong immune system—for both of you. Your baby's tiny tummy is still learning how to digest, and your gut health can even shape your baby's developing gut.

Simple Gut-Friendly Hacks for Moms:

1. Listen to your gut: Your gut speaks more than you realize. That flutter before a decision, the feeling of fullness, or that quiet nudge when something feels off—it's all your second brain trying to guide you. Trust it.

2. Eat rainbow foods: Include a variety of fruits, veggies, and whole grains. The more colors on your plate, the happier your gut bugs will be.

3. Add probiotics and prebiotics: Yogurt, bananas, garlic, and fermented foods (like pickles or buttermilk) help grow good bacteria.

4. Use healing spices: Turmeric, cumin, ginger, and fenugreek support digestion and help reduce inflammation.

5. Drink enough water: Staying hydrated helps your gut process food and absorb nutrients.

6. Cut down sugar and processed foods: Too much sugar can harm your gut bacteria and affect your mood.

Gut and Sleep: A Two-Way Street

Now, here's something most people don't know—your gut and sleep are deeply connected.

Just one sleepless night can upset your gut bacteria, mess with your hunger hormones, and leave you moody, bloated, and low on energy.

I remember being a new mom, running on broken sleep. I had dark circles, constant bloating, and my body just felt… off. I thought it was just the baby waking up at night.

But then I noticed a habit: I was always on my phone.

Every time I woke up, I'd scroll through social media. I thought it helped me pass the time.

But in truth, it was hurting me.

I didn't know that the blue light from my screen was messing with my sleep.

It disrupted melatonin production—the sleep hormone often called the "vampire hormone" because it works best in darkness. Sleep-deprived, I felt like a vampire myself—awake at night, drained during the day.

When I slowly replaced my night-time scrolling with breathing exercises or soft music, something shifted. No, I didn't magically turn into a glowing goddess—but I felt calmer, more grounded. My gut felt lighter. My mood improved. I was less snappy. I felt more like… me.

Simple Sleep Hacks for Exhausted Moms:

1. Nap when your baby naps—even 15 minutes helps.

2. Limit screens before bedtime.

3. Create a cozy, dim space for sleep.

4. Avoid caffeine and sugar after sunset.

5. Ask for help. Share night duties if you can.

6. Use white noise to calm both you and your baby.

7. Choose rest over chores—healing is a priority.

8. Don't chase perfect sleep. Rest when you can. Be kind to yourself.

Let the Sun In: Nature's Sleep Reset

One of the most beautiful shifts came when I started stepping out for morning sunlight.

Dr. Andrew Huberman, a neuroscientist, says in his podcast that just 5–10 minutes of sunlight in the morning helps reset your body clock. It helps you sleep better at night and feel more awake in the day.

You don't have to go for a long walk. Just open the window. Stand on your balcony. Step out with your baby for a few minutes.

That sunlight tells your body: It's morning, you're safe, and you can start fresh.

Your gut and your sleep are powerful healing tools.

They affect your mood, your energy, your milk, your baby, and your joy.

You don't have to do it all perfectly.

But with a little love, sunlight, and rest, your body can begin to heal from the inside out.

Your second brain is listening. Feed it gently. Nurture it kindly.

And it will take care of both of you.

Just like your gut brain, the little brain in your heart deserves love and care too.

Because the heart isn't just fuel for your body—

It's where your core emotions begin. It's where intuition speaks.

Take care of your Little Brain: The Heart-Brain

Have you ever woken up just before your baby cried? Or felt a strong urge to check on them—only to find it was the right time?

That's your mommy instinct.

And much of that inner knowing flows from your heart.

But instincts can sometimes be clouded—by fear, exhaustion, or too much noise in the mind.

That's where heart-brain coherence helps.

It teaches you to pause, breathe, and respond—not react. It gently brings you back to what truly matters.

Simple Techniques for Heart-Brain Coherence:

1. Heart-focused breathing: Breathe slowly and gently, focusing on the area around your heart.

2. Positive emotions: Think of a person, pet, place, or memory that fills you with love or joy. Let it warm your heart.

3. Gratitude journaling: Write down three things you're grateful for—big or small.

4. Nature time: Step outside, sit under a tree, feel the breeze. Let nature hold you.

5. Guided visualization: Picture yourself enjoying little moments with your baby. Feel it with all your senses.

6. Use heart rhythm apps (if available): Tools that track your heart coherence can help you stay in sync with yourself.

A Gentle Heart Ritual curated for Moms:

Find a quiet moment—maybe while your baby is resting. Sit or lie down comfortably. Relax your shoulders.

Place your left hand over your own heart, and your right hand gently on your baby's chest.

Close your eyes. Feel your heartbeat—strong, steady.

Now feel your baby's heartbeat—tiny, quick, and full of life.

Two rhythms. Two hearts. One bond.

Take a slow, deep breath in. And as you exhale, feel your body soften.

Think about the love that brought you here.

The strength of your mother, your grandmother, and all the women before you. Their heartbeat carried you—just like yours now carries your baby.

Their courage lives in you. Their ancestral wisdom echoes in every beat.

Let that love rise in your chest.

Let it flow through your hand into your baby.

Whisper a blessing, a gentle wish, or simply say:

"I love you. I'm here. You are safe."

Stay in this quiet moment for as long as you wish.

Let the connection fill you with peace.

Let your heart speak—and listen.

But remember—these hacks and techniques only work when they're planted deep into your subconscious mind. That's why caring for your subconscious brain is so important.

Take Care of Your Subconscious Brain:

No matter how much effort you put into caring for your brain, if you keep slipping back into old habits, it's easy to fall into the same cycle of stress or exhaustion.

To break free, you need to create new habits—and gently feed them into your subconscious until they become automatic.

Because once your subconscious mind changes, everything around you begin to change.

Think of it like updating your phone's software. To make it run better, you need to clear old bugs and install new updates.

Your brain works the same way. You have to *"unlearn"* habits that no longer serve you and make space for the ones that do.

You can't fill a cup that's already full.

This doesn't mean forgetting your past. It means choosing new patterns that support your well-being—and repeating them until they become your new normal.

Yes, old habits may resurface now and then. And that's okay. What matters is that you keep moving forward.

For new moms, everything can feel new and overwhelming at first. But slowly, with small steps, even the most tiring tasks can become automatic and easeful.

Simple Ways to Train Your Subconscious and Build Helpful Habits:

1. **Repeat, repeat, repeat:** The more you do something, the more your brain wires it in. Daily baby care like feeding, bathing, or bedtime will soon feel like second nature.

2. **Create routines:** A predictable schedule helps your mind (and your baby's) feel safe and settled. Routines build structure and reduce mental load.

3. **Stay present:** Try to be mindful during everyday tasks. Notice how things feel. This awareness helps your brain form stronger habit loops.

4. **Learn and adjust:** Every baby is different. Trust that over time, you'll understand your child better—and things will get easier.

5. **Use visual cues:** Sticky notes, checklists, or reminders can gently guide your actions until the habits stick.

6. **Break it down:** Big tasks feel lighter when you split them into tiny steps. Even laying out baby clothes the night before can bring calm to your morning.

7. Celebrate small wins: Each time you follow through with a new habit, take a moment to feel proud. Tiny victories fuel lasting change.

8. Lean on others: Share your journey with other moms or trusted people. You're not alone—and sometimes a tip or a kind word makes all the difference.

And most importantly, trust the process.

It might take time—but be patient with yourself.

Day by day, it gets better.

And soon, your brain will begin to work with you, not against you.

To keep your subconscious mind on track, these simple yet powerful mind-and-body hacks can work wonders. One mindful baby step at a time, you'll begin to feel more grounded, more energized, and more connected to yourself.

Hacks for Mind and Body

Balancing motherhood with self-care can be tough. But with small, intentional shifts, you can begin to nurture both your mind and body in gentle, lasting ways.

Mind Hacks:

1. The Humming Effect: Try humming or soft chanting to stay grounded. You don't have to be religious—just notice how a gentle "shh" soothes your baby or how a firm "No" grabs attention. Sound has power. Its vibration calms the mind, settles the body, and brings you into the present moment. Even a lullaby might work wonders.

2. Affirmations: Speak to yourself with kindness. Words like "I am doing my best" or "I am a loving, capable mom" help rebuild emotional strength and self-trust.

3. Creative Outlets: Drawing, journaling, crafting—anything that lets you express yourself—can offer emotional release and bring tiny sparks of joy.

4. Growth Mindset: Every challenge is an opportunity to learn. Embracing a growth mindset builds resilience and helps you stay afloat when the waves of motherhood get rough.

Body Hacks:

1. Comfortable Clothing: Wear what feels good on your skin and allows you to move freely. Feeling physically comfortable supports emotional ease.

2. Baby Wearing: Using a sling keeps your baby close while freeing your hands. It's a small shift that makes a big difference.

3. Massage & Self-Care: A warm bath or a gentle massage can help melt stress and soothe your body.

4. Time Outdoors: Step outside. Fresh air and sunlight can lift your spirits, clear your mind, and give you a reset.

Remember: Taking care of yourself isn't a luxury—it's essential. When you care for your body and mind, you're also caring for your baby.

Exercise Hacks

Movement, when done mindfully, can gently recharge your brain and body health.

After giving birth, it's normal to feel disconnected from your body. It may look and feel unfamiliar—and that's okay. Your body has done something incredible. It deserves love, not pressure.

Exercise isn't about "bouncing back." It's about feeling stronger, calmer, and more alive. Moving your body—even for just a few minutes—can lift your mood, ease stress, and improve sleep.

Some days, just carrying your baby is enough. Other days, you might find a moment to stretch or walk. Every bit counts.

Even a few minutes of strength training per week can improve energy, mood, and metabolic health—without hours at the gym (Body by Science, McGuff & Little, 2009).

Gentle Ways to Move Your Body:

1. Start Slow: Try 10–15 minutes of stretching or gentle yoga to build strength gradually.

2. Involve Your Baby: Hold or carry your baby while doing light movements or tummy time exercises.

3. Use Nap Time Wisely: Try a short workout video or stretch during nap time.

4. Step Outside: A short walk with your baby can refresh your mind and body.

5. Move at Home: Use simple exercises like squats or stretches—no equipment needed.

6. Play Actively: Dance, crawl, or roll around with your baby during playtime.

7. Add Movement to Chores: Sneak in stretches or squats while cooking or folding clothes.

8. Find Support: Join a mom-and-baby group for encouragement—online or locally.

9. Stay Flexible: Some days will be harder. Do what you can, and be kind to yourself.

10. Use Baby Carriers: Move gently with your baby in a carrier for added connection and resistance.

Remember, these are not rules—they are gentle invitations to reconnect with your body.

Start small. But start smart.

Now, let's go even deeper—into the heart of real healing.

This is where true brain care begins—not just with physical habits or mindful practices, but with something much deeper. Soul care. The kind of care that heals from within.

And here's one of the most powerful, yet often forgotten tools for that kind of healing:

A Final Secret Hack: Laughter

Yes, laughter.

How long has it been since you truly laughed? The kind of laughter that makes your eyes water and your belly hurt?

If your answer is "too long" or "I can't remember," then you might be missing something with near-magical powers.

Laughter isn't just fun—it's healing. It's your body's natural medicine.

It helps release feel-good chemicals like endorphins, oxytocin, serotonin, and dopamine. These helps reduce stress, lift your mood, ease pain, and create a sense of connection.

When you laugh, your body relaxes. Your mind lets go. Your heart opens.

Why Laughter Heals

- **It reduces stress:** Laughing melts tension. Even tough moments feel a little lighter.

- **It lifts your mood:** A giggle can shift your emotional state in seconds.

- **It deepens connection:** Laughing with someone—your partner, your friend, your baby—creates closeness.

- **It boosts confidence:** It helps you feel more at ease, especially around others.

- **It brings physical relief:** Deep laughter can ease pain and help you sleep better.

Laughter—A Real-Life Doctor

One of the most powerful examples is a writer named Norman Cousins. In the 1960s, he was diagnosed with a painful, incurable disease called ankylosing spondylitis.

Instead of giving up, he tried something different: large doses of vitamin C… and **comedy**.

He watched funny movies and shows, laughing as much as possible. He found that ten minutes of deep belly laughter gave him two hours of pain-free sleep. Over time, he began to heal—not just emotionally, but physically.

He later wrote a book, Anatomy of an Illness, sharing how his positive attitude and laughter played a powerful role in his recovery.

My Own Laughter Doctor:

For me, my laughter doctor came in the form of a TV show—*The Big Bang Theory*.

Just like the universe began with a Big Bang, my healing began with laughter from that show. Every giggle, every chuckle helped me breathe a little easier, feel a little stronger.

Let Joy In:

Laugh with your baby. Watch something silly. Call a friend who makes you smile. Find your little daily dose of joy.

Laughter doesn't just make life more fun—it helps you heal, feel, and connect.

Let joy be part of your self-care.

Let laughter be your medicine.

Quick Summary for Mommy Brain Boosters:

- **Brain Hacks:** Build healthy habits, stay mentally engaged.
- **Take Care of Your Second Brain (Gut):** Eat well to improve your mood, energy, and overall health.
- **Take Care of Your Sleep:** Prioritize sleep, hydration, and brain-boosting foods to fuel your brain.
- **Listen to Your Heart:** Connect emotionally with your baby, stay calm and balanced.
- **Soothe Your Subconscious Brain:** Be kind to yourself, address stress, and clear your mind.
- **Mind and Body Care:** Move gently, and relax to nourish both body and mind.
- **Laugh Out to Heal and Bond:** Let laughter heal and deepen your bond with your baby.

Up next is a simple assessment to reflect on your journey—your sleep, nutrition, emotional well-being, and self-compassion. Use it to check in, celebrate your progress, and gently realign where needed.

Mommy Brain Boosters Assessment Worksheet

Before you begin, remember that this is your moment to pause and reflect. Be honest, be kind, and remember—this is not a test. There are no right or wrong answers, only insights to gently guide you toward growth, healing, and self-care.

1. Brain Health:

1. How often do you engage in activities that stimulate your brain (e.g., reading, puzzles, or learning new skills)?

a) Daily

b) A few times a week

c) Rarely

d) Never

2. How often do you eat foods that are good for brain health, like fatty fish, nuts, or seeds?

a) Daily

b) A few times a week

c) Rarely

d) Never

3. Do you feel mentally alert and focused during the day?

a) Always

b) Sometimes

c) Rarely

d) Never

2. Gut Health:

1. How often do you consume fiber-rich foods (e.g., fruits, vegetables, whole grains)?

a) Daily

b) A few times a week

c) Rarely

d) Never

2. How often do you eat probiotics or fermented foods (e.g., yogurt, kimchi)?

a) Daily

b) A few times a week

c) Rarely

d) Never

3. Do you experience digestive discomfort (e.g., bloating, gas, constipation)?

a) Never

b) Occasionally

c) Frequently

d) Always

3. Sleep Hygiene:

1. How often do you follow a consistent sleep routine (e.g., going to bed at the same time each night)?

a) Always

b) Sometimes

c) Rarely

d) Never

2. How often do you wake up feeling refreshed and well-rested?

a) Always

b) Sometimes

c) Rarely

d) Never

3. How often do you experience trouble falling asleep or staying asleep?

a) Never

b) Occasionally

c) Frequently

d) Always

4. What was your sleep pattern before pregnancy?

a) Healthy and regular

b) Irregular but manageable

c) Frequent disturbances or poor quality

d) I can't remember

4. Heart Health:

1. How often do you engage in activities that raise your heart rate (e.g., walking, jogging, or dancing)?

a) Daily

b) A few times a week

c) Rarely

d) Never

2. Do you eat foods that are good for heart health (e.g., fruits, vegetables, healthy fats)?

a) Always

b) Sometimes

c) Rarely

d) Never

3. Do you feel your heart rate increase with stress or anxiety?

a) Never

b) Occasionally

c) Frequently

d) Always

5. Subconscious Habits:

1. How often do you catch yourself overthinking or stressing about situations?

a) Rarely

b) Sometimes

c) Often

d) Always

2. How often do you engage in unhealthy eating habits (e.g., overeating, emotional eating)?

a) Rarely

b) Sometimes

c) Often

d) Always

3. Do you have habits that drain your energy, like negative thinking or excessive screen time?

a) Never

b) Occasionally

c) Frequently

d) Always

6. Exercise:

1. How often do you engage in physical exercise or movement (e.g., walking, yoga, stretching)?

a) Daily

b) A few times a week

c) Rarely

d) Never

2. How do you feel about your current level of physical activity?

a) Satisfied and energized

b) Neutral

c) Unsatisfied and tired

d) Very unsatisfied and inactive

3. How much do you enjoy being physically active?

a) Very much

b) Somewhat

c) Not much

d) Not at all

7. Willingness to Change Unhealthy Habits:

1. How willing are you to change unhealthy habits for the sake of your well-being?

a) Very willing

b) Somewhat willing

c) Neutral

d) Not willing

2. Have you noticed any specific habits that drain you or affect your well-being? (e.g., overthinking, overeating, poor sleep)

a) Yes, and I am actively trying to change them

b) Yes, but I haven't started to change them yet

c) No, I haven't noticed any

d) Not sure

3. How likely are you to seek support or resources to improve your habits?

a) Very likely

b) Likely

c) Unlikely

d) Very unlikely

Final Reflection:

1. What is one area you feel most drawn to improve right now?

2. How do you think nurturing this area could support your well-being?

3. What small positive changes have you already noticed?

Self-Assessment:

1. How satisfied are you with your answers?

a) Very satisfied

b) Satisfied

c) Neutral

d) Unsatisfied

2. How would you describe where you are on your brain care journey?

a) I feel empowered and am actively growing

b) I'm aware of what I need and taking small steps

c) I'm just beginning to explore and understand

d) I'm unsure, but open to learning and evolving

Your Brain Care Progress Card:

After answering the questions, rate each area from 1 to 10, with 1 being poor and 10 being excellent.

1. Overall Brain Health Score: ___/10

2. Gut Health Score: ___/10

3. Sleep Quality Score: ___/10

4. Heart Health Score: ___/10

5. Subconscious Habits Score: ___/10

6. Exercise Score: ___/10

How to Rate Yourself:

•1-3: Needs significant improvement

• 4-6: Somewhat healthy but requires more focus and care

• 7-9: Good, with minor adjustments needed for optimal health

• 10: Excellent, on track and thriving

Now that you've completed the assessment, you've a clearer picture of where you stand. These scores are just a starting point of your brain care journey. Focus on the areas that matter most to you, and take small, meaningful steps to create lasting change.

Up next: The 5 Golden Rules for Brain Health. Think of them as headlights lighting your path and airbags cushioning your ride—tools to help you grow, heal, and thrive as both a mother and a person.

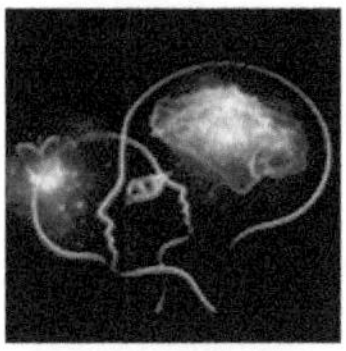

CHAPTER 10

THE 5 GOLDEN RULES FOR BRAIN HEALTH

Our brain likes to follow rules. And for most of our lives, we've been following the ones that were silently programmed into our mental software long ago.

Now, it's time to update that software.

But this time—it's in *your* hands.

These five golden rules aren't about becoming someone else. They're about bringing out the authenticity within you.

They help you evolve into a stronger, more empowered version of yourself.

For example, you can slowly replace fear and guilt with love and courage.

Your Body, Your Brain, Your Rules

Imagine your body as a colony of trillions of tiny workers—your cells—each busily doing its job. These workers follow simple rules to keep everything running smoothly.

Just as the heart doesn't take on the lungs' job and follows its own rules, every part of your body, including your brain, has its guiding principles.

These five golden rules for brain health are gentle reminders—tools to help you feel more balanced, in control, and mentally nourished.

They don't have to be followed perfectly. They're not about pressure; they're about peace.

And with that, let's explore the first golden rule:

1. Balance: The Bridge Between Chaos and Peace

Balance is key to your brain's health. It's what keeps your body and mind working smoothly—a state that is called *homeostasis.* It simply means your brain and body are in sync, working together to keep you calm, clear-headed, and ready for whatever life brings.

Now imagine a see-saw. Some days, you're on the go—doing everything, pushing through, getting things done. Other days, all your body wants is to rest. But if you push too much, you burn out. If you rest too long, you feel stuck.

The secret is in finding the sweet spot—where effort and rest support each other, keeping you steady.

Choose your side consciously:

With all the chaos around us, slipping into stress mode becomes easy. That's your sympathetic nervous system—the body's "fight or flight" side. But the moment you become aware of it, you gain the power to gently shift to the other side—the parasympathetic nervous system—the one that brings calm, healing, and peace.

Imagine kids playing on a see-saw. If one child pushes too hard or jumps off suddenly, the other gets hurt. But when both kids understand the rhythm—when to go up, when to come down—it becomes fun. Smooth. Joyful. That's how balance should feel in your life. Not forced. Not one-sided. Just a gentle back-and-forth—a playful ride between effort and ease.

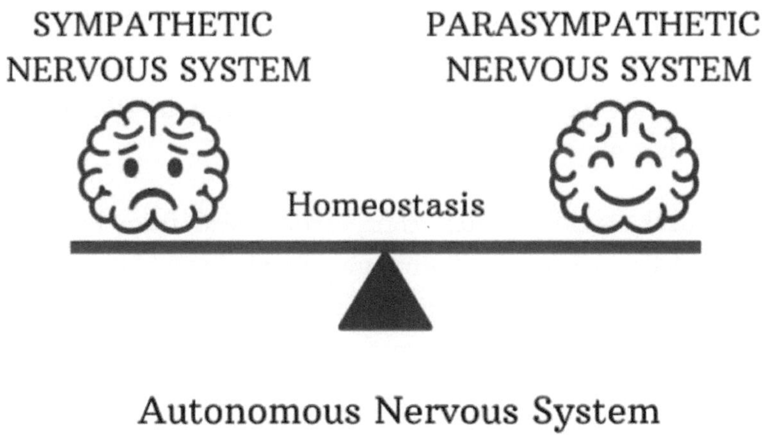

It's not about staying on one side forever. It's about knowing when to shift, and how to shift—gently, not harshly.

And it starts with one simple thing—listening to your body and honoring what it needs. Without guilt. Without pressure.

Once you learn this dance, your brain starts to feel lighter, clearer, and more at peace.

Now that you've felt the power of balance, let's move to the next golden rule—**the powerful role of hormones**, those invisible messengers that shape your emotions, energy, and inner world.

2. Hormonal Harmony: The Dopamine Dilemma

Understand and support your hormones—they're the emotional compass of your motherhood journey.

The other day, Neerja, a mother of two—one toddler and one teenager—sat on the couch, completely drained. Her baby was finally asleep, but instead of resting, her eyes were glued to her phone. She had been scrolling for over an hour—lost in a sea of reels, online offers, and endless content.

In the background, her teenage son yelled from his room, "Ugh! The data's over!"—frustrated mid-game. She sighed, refilled the internet pack again, and heard the usual, "Just one more game, Ma."

It's not just Neerja. These days, many of us find our children glued to their screens, eyes locked in, chasing digital wins. That's the hormone *dopamine* at work—just in a different form. It's the same loop of seeking rewards, escaping boredom, and craving that next little hit of pleasure.

Dr. Anna Lembke, in her book *Dopamine Nation*, calls dopamine **"the new currency."**

What we often don't realize is—both adults and children are caught in this hormonal cycle, led by *dopamine*—the brain's "reward chemical." It lights up when we do something that feels good: ticking off a to-do, buying something new, getting a compliment, or receiving a 'like' on a post. Without dopamine, we wouldn't even feel the drive to eat, move, or connect.

Think of the thrill of online shopping, or how often we instinctively reach for our phones. Every ping, every discount, every "you saved 50%" message is designed to give your brain a little dopamine high.

Brain Trap

Supermarkets, apps, social media—they all know how to trigger our reward system. That's how binge-watching happens. That's how emotional spending or late-night scrolling becomes a habit. It's not about weak willpower—it's just how our brains are wired.

How many times have you bought something impulsively, only to regret it later?

This is what David T. Courtwright calls *"limbic capitalism"*—a world where industries feed on our emotions to keep us hooked, consuming more, scrolling longer, and craving endlessly. Over time, this loop can quietly lead to addiction.

Motherhood and Dopamine

In motherhood, dopamine is released in the most soulful, grounding moments—when your baby breastfeeds, when they smile for the first time, when they stop crying in your arms. These are the deep, natural highs that fill your heart and calm your spirit. They're not ***reel-istic***—but they are ***real-istic***.

But in today's noisy, overstimulated world, our natural reward system gets hijacked. We're surrounded by endless dopamine triggers—likes, flash sales, fast food, reels, video games. And slowly, our brain starts mistaking quick hits of pleasure for true happiness.

Here's why:

The brain can only handle so much stimulation. When pleasure comes too often, too fast, it adapts by lowering your dopamine baseline.

Now, you need more to feel less.

What once made you smile barely registers.

What once gave you peace now feels dull. That's when the reward system starts to feel… broken.

Think about the first-time thrills:

Your first job.

Your first love.

Your first success.

That high? It felt magical. But try chasing that same feeling again—it's harder to reach. That's dopamine adaptation. The baseline shifts.

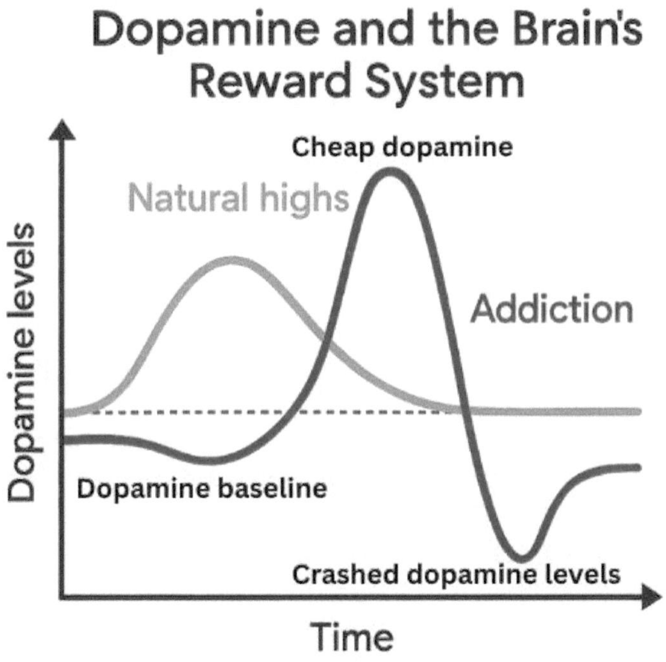

DOPAMINE DETOX: A Gentle Reset

Thankfully, the brain has a beautiful ability—it can reset.

And here's the fascinating part: our brain processes both pain and pleasure in the same area (*Dopamine Nation*—Dr. Anna Lembke). To feel one, the other must exist.

It reminds us of those wise old truths—

To know light, we must experience the dark.

To appreciate the day, we must pass through the night.

It's nature's way of restoring balance.

When we flood our brain with too much pleasure—too often—it's like sitting on one end of a seesaw and piling on more and more weight.

Eventually, it tips too far.

The joy dulls, and discomfort sneaks in to even things out.

That's why after a binge—whether it's sweets, screens, or shopping—you feel tired, restless, or even sad.

To feel balanced again, we need to gently remove those extra weights.

That's when the magic happens: the seesaw begins to shift back.

The brain resets.

That's the heart of a *dopamine detox*—not to give up joy, but to rediscover it.

Not to punish yourself, but to find balance again.

How to do it:

Start small.

Maybe it's a day without Instagram. Or a walk instead of an online scroll. These small pauses reset your brain's rhythm.

Dopamine detox is a game-changing golden rule—and one that every new mom can deeply relate to.

It helps you reconnect with real joy and emotional clarity.

But once the mental fog begins to lift, something deeper often comes into focus—those silent, stubborn beliefs that quietly hold you back.

That brings us to the next golden rule: breaking free from mental monsters.

Because sometimes, it's not just hormones or habits that weigh you down—it's the inner voice shaped by years of conditioning.

And unless we face these "mental monsters," we stay stuck in patterns that no longer serve us.

3. Break Free from Mental Monsters

With the arrival of your bundle of joy comes a new bundle of emotional baggage—filled with self-doubt, fears, and beliefs that may resurface, holding you back once again.

These "mental monsters" don't appear overnight; they've been shaped over years of conditioning. Though they are not set in stone, they can feel deeply wired—silently shaping how you think, decide, and live.

Over time, they settle into the deepest corners of our minds, subtly influencing the way we think, decide and live.

"You're not good enough," whispers one voice.

"You should be doing more," or "You should be like her," echoes another.

But what if that voice isn't truly yours?

What if it's just a reflection of **outdated expectations and borrowed beliefs**?

Recognizing these mental monsters is the first step toward breaking free.

Conquering the Mental Monsters: Change Your Perception

Start by noticing when a belief feels heavy—when it holds you back instead of lifting you up.

Observe your thoughts.

Are they empowering? Or are they quietly weighing you down?

For instance, if you feel guilty for taking a break, pause and ask: Why do I believe this?

Maybe it's because you were taught that rest equals laziness.

Challenge it.

Then replace it with a belief that serves you better: Rest fuels resilience.

Changing your perception doesn't happen overnight—it's a gentle, ongoing process.

It's like opening the window in a stuffy room. Slowly, light and fresh air begin to pour in.

Remember: Removing mental barriers isn't just about breaking free.

It's about reclaiming your power—your voice, your truth, your joy.

Every time you challenge a mental monster, you create space for your true self to shine through—a mom who is not just surviving, but thriving.

Now that you've begun to break free from mental barriers, the next golden rule is learning how to protect your sacred energy and well-being by setting healthy boundaries—starting with the powerful act of saying 'no.'

Because by mastering the art of saying no, you create the space your brain and body need to breathe, reset, and truly heal.

4. Learn to Say 'No': Saying 'No' is Saying 'Yes' to Your Brain Health (Break free)

As a new mom, one of the most powerful ways to protect your mental and emotional well-being is by learning how to say **'no.'**

We're often pressured to say **'yes'**—to social invites, unsolicited advice, family obligations, or unrealistic expectations. But trying to please everyone can leave you feeling drained, overwhelmed, and disconnected from what truly matters.

Saying 'no' isn't selfish—it's self-protection. It's about setting healthy boundaries so you can care for yourself and your baby with intention.

In the book *The Art of Saying No*, there's a powerful truth:

"Every time you say 'yes' to something, you are saying 'no' to something else."

So, when you say yes to hosting dinner while sleep-deprived, you're also saying no to your rest, your baby, and your peace.

Saying 'no' isn't rejection. It's redirection.

Redirected toward your energy, your clarity, and your healing.

How to Say 'No' With Confidence

1. **Be honest and kind:** "Thank you for asking, but I can't commit right now."

2. **Pause before responding:** Ask yourself, "Will this nourish me or exhaust me?"

3. **Seek support:** Talk to someone you trust before making decisions.

Every 'no' creates space—for what truly matters:

Your well-being. Your bond. Your brain.

Now that you've experienced the power of saying 'no' and setting boundaries, it's time to embrace the next golden rule—clearing out the mental clutter that no longer serves you in your journey as a mom.

5. The Art of Letting Go: Declutter Your Mental Space

In autumn, trees don't cling to their leaves. Through a gentle process called *abscission*, they release what they no longer need—drawing nutrients back to their roots, preserving what matters most, and preparing for new growth.

Motherhood is your autumn.

A season of change, of realignment, and of choosing what to carry forward.

When your baby arrived, your home likely changed.

Furniture was rearranged. Closets were cleared. Space was made for what truly matters.

I remember a friend who had to let go of her favorite armchair—a cozy spot she'd loved for years. But as her baby's crib arrived, she knew it was time to release the familiar to make space for something new.

Your mind, like your home, also needs this kind of intentional reset.

Over time, it fills with thoughts, beliefs, and habits that may have once served you—but now weigh you down. Motherhood offers a powerful invitation to pause and ask:

What mental clutter am I still holding onto?

Does it serve me—or hold me back?

Sometimes, old beliefs live in our minds rent-free.

Like the thought: "I have to do everything perfectly."

Pause. Ask yourself:

Where did this come from?

Is it truly mine—or something passed down, picked up, or shaped by someone else's story?

Then, gently reframe it:

"I'm learning, growing, and showing up—and that's more than enough."

Letting go doesn't mean giving up.

It means making space for growth, clarity, and calm.

Learn from the Best: Nature

Just like trees instinctively know when to let go, we too hold that inner wisdom.

But unlike trees, we don't shed our emotional burdens automatically.

We carry them—often silently—unaware of how much they're costing us.

Here's the good news:

Your brain can prune old patterns—consciously.

This process is known as ***neural pruning***.

It's how your brain eliminates connections that are no longer useful, freeing up space for healthier, more empowering beliefs.

Think of it as gardening for your mind.

Art of Letting
"GO"

Abcission in trees **Conscious Neural Pruning**

Start by noticing the thoughts that drain you.

The beliefs that make you feel anxious, small, or stuck.

Then choose to let them go.

As you gently replace them with healthier ones, your brain will do the rest—

Weakening the old, strengthening the new.

Over time, you're not just decluttering.

You're rewiring.

There's a saying in neuroscience:

"Neurons that fire together, wire together."

The more you nurture positive, empowering thoughts, the stronger those neural pathways become.

So, keep tending to your inner garden.

Let the old fall away.

You're creating fertile ground for who you're becoming—One beautiful, conscious choice at a time.

Quick Summary of the 5 Golden Rules:

Here's a quick recap of the five golden rules for brain health:

- Balance: Create harmony between your body, mind, and emotions. A balanced mind leads to a balanced life.

- Hormonal Harmony: Understand and support your body's hormonal changes to maintain emotional stability.

- Removing Mental Barriers: Overcome limiting beliefs and fears that hold you back from living your best life.

• Learning to Say 'No': Protect your time and energy by setting healthy boundaries. Saying no is an act of self-care.

• The Art of Letting Go: Clear mental clutter and let go of habits that no longer serve you, making space for growth and peace.

> *When your brain feels foggy, overwhelmed, or disconnected, return to these five golden rules. They're not checkboxes—they're gentle reminders. Start small. Choose balance. Honor your hormones. Question old beliefs. Say no when you must. And let go of what's no longer yours to carry. You're not just healing your brain—you're building a new world for you and your child.*

By living these golden rules, you're not just nurturing your brain—you're becoming something greater:

A more powerful, present, and peaceful version of yourself. Someone who creates a loving environment where your child can grow, feel safe, and see the world through a lens of hope and possibility.

Now that you've embraced the five golden rules, it's time to take the next step—unlocking the power that already lives within you.

What comes next will equip you with the tools and insights to support your journey—not just as a mother, but as a woman and a holistic being.

Because what lies ahead isn't just about making motherhood easier—it's about rising into a wiser, stronger version of yourself, with a deeper awareness that will guide you through every season of life.

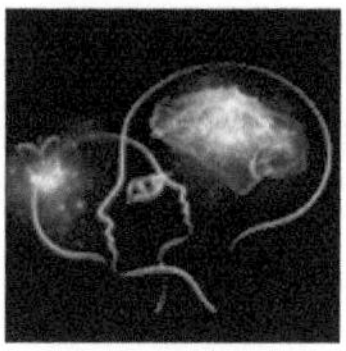

CHAPTER 11

UNLOCK YOUR TRUE POTENTIAL

Once you've baby-proofed your brain by applying the insights from the previous chapters, it's time to take the next leap—unlocking your true potential.

The First Baby Steps Toward Your True Potential

The steps ahead may seem simple—but they're not always easy, especially when your world revolves around your baby's needs and an endless to-do list.

But just like your baby's first steps—where they fall, rise, and try again—you'll rise too.

Each attempt rewires your brain. Each step builds strength. And with every stumble, you're getting closer to something extraordinary.

This journey begins with four key steps, held together by a gentle yet powerful framework called MIRA:

Meditation, Introspection, Reflection, and Adaptation.

These four pillars will guide you toward a deeper connection—with yourself, with your child, and with life itself.

The MIRA Framework: Your Path to Inner Growth

Let's begin with the first—and most grounding—step.

Meditation: The Key to Unlock Your Brain's Treasure

Meditation isn't just a practice—it's a gentle shift.

It changes the way you think, feel, and respond to life.

It builds calm, clarity, and resilience—like an emergency toolkit for your mind, ready to help you stay grounded in tough moments.

As a mom, one of the best gifts you can give your child is the habit of meditation.

Children don't always listen to what we say—but they absorb what we do.

When they see you taking time to breathe and be still, it plants a seed.

Maybe they won't use it now, but one day—when life gets hard—they'll remember.

Meditation is like medicine for your soul.

It soothes your thoughts, your heart, and even your body.

It opens a door to healing and helps you see new possibilities you never noticed before.

Yes, it takes time. And yes, it may feel like one more thing on your to-do list.

But the truth?

Meditation doesn't take your time—it gives it back—through better focus, more energy, and a clearer mind.

The key is mindfulness—being aware of what you feed your mind and body.

Because everything you take in—whether it's food, thoughts, or emotions—shapes how you feel.

Meditation didn't change my life overnight.

It took practice. And patience. And showing up even when I didn't feel like it.

But it changed everything.

Now, let's begin with a simple, gentle guide to help you start—without overwhelm.

Steps to Start Meditation

1. Shift Your Brain State:

Begin by calming your mind with slow, deep breaths.

With each breath, your brain shifts from the active beta state (where thoughts are racing), to the calm alpha state, and finally into the deeply restful theta state.

This theta state—often called Yoga Nidra or "non-sleep deep rest" (NSDR), as mentioned by Dr. Andrew Huberman—is where emotional healing begins and creativity flows.

It's the perfect space to rewire your thoughts and restore your energy.

Tip: Try listening to theta wave music with headphones to help ease into this state.

Once you're there, gently start visualizing your goals and dreams. This is where your mind becomes a tool for creating the life you want.

2. Visualize:

Once your brain is calm, it's time to guide it toward what you want most.

Close your eyes and picture the life you want to live.

See yourself bonding with your child—handling daily chaos with calm and grace.

Feel peace, even during stressful moments.

Visualization isn't just wishful thinking—it's powerful mental training.

Take actor Jim Carrey, for example.

Long before he found success, he wrote himself a multimillion-dollar check and kept it in his wallet as a reminder of his dream.

He visualized his success daily—until it became real.

Many athletes do the same—mentally rehearsing their victory before they ever step into the game.

Now do the same for your day—visualize it unfolding exactly how you want.

Let your mind rehearse peace, joy, and confidence before the world even asks you to show up.

3. Self-Hypnosis:

Self-hypnosis is the practice of planting positive, empowering thoughts in your mind. Say to yourself:

- "I am confident."
- "I am calm."
- "I can handle anything."

These affirmations may seem simple—but when repeated with belief and emotion, they begin to rewire your brain for calm, confidence, and clarity.

Be specific. The more vivid and personal your affirmations, the deeper they resonate.

And most importantly—***feel*** your affirmations. Without intention and emotion, they're just empty words.

Your feeling is the energy that fuels transformation. It's the secret ingredient that helps your goals take root and manifest.

4. Avoid Negativity: The Power of Mirror Neurons

Have you ever cried after watching a heartbreaking news story or a dramatic movie?

Even though you weren't there—your body reacted. Your eyes welled up, your chest tightened, and your emotions felt real.

Why does that happen?

The answer lies in something remarkable: ***mirror neurons.***

These special cells in your brain allow you to feel what others feel.

When you see someone in pain, your mirror neurons fire as if you're experiencing it too.

It's your brain's way of creating empathy, bonding, and shared emotion.

It's also why a simple smile can lift your mood—and why constant exposure to stress or negativity can weigh you down.

Your Brain is Like a Sponge

Your mind absorbs everything around you—even the things you don't consciously focus on.

And what's even more fascinating?

Your brain often can't tell the difference between what's real and what's imagined.

So, when you're repeatedly exposed to negativity—be it from media, toxic conversations, or past memories—your brain reacts as if it's under threat.

Stress hormones rise.

You slip into fight-or-flight mode.

You carry tension that was never truly yours to begin with.

What You Feed Your Mind Matters: So In, So Out

That's why it's so important to be mindful of what you allow into your inner world.

When you choose to limit negativity, you send your brain a clear signal:

"I'm safe. I'm calm."

This single shift changes how you feel—and how you show up in life every day.

Your Emotions Shape Your Baby's World

Now here's where it gets truly powerful.

When you smile at your baby, their mirror neurons light up. They absorb your calm, your joy, your love.

But if they sense stress, frustration, or anxiety, they absorb that too.

You're not just caring for your own emotional well-being—you're shaping the emotional landscape of your child's developing brain.

So, the question becomes:

What do you want your child to mirror?

Your peace, presence, and joy?

Or your worry, stress, and overwhelm?

Reset Through Meditation

Meditation gives your brain the break it needs. It helps calm your nervous system, reset your emotional state, and bring you back to balance.

When you meditate, you're not just helping yourself—you're creating a ripple effect of calm.

Your calm becomes your child's calm.

And once this becomes part of your rhythm, you're ready for the next step: ***introspection***—your most powerful tool for unlocking your true potential.

Introspection: The Quiet Strength of Understanding Yourself

Now that you've practiced meditation, shifted your brain state, visualized, and affirmed your inner strength, it's time to gently tune in—deeply—to how your body and emotions respond.

With each deep breath, bring your attention to different parts of yourself. Think of it like checking in with an old friend—just noticing how you feel, both physically and emotionally.

Introspection is simply looking inward.

It's like pausing on a busy day to ask yourself:

"How does my body feel right now?"

"Is my chest tight or relaxed?"

"Are my shoulders tense or at ease? What emotions am I feeling? What truly matters to me at this moment?"

This quiet practice helps you connect more deeply with your emotions and understand how you respond to the world around you. By listening to your body, you become more in tune with your true needs.

Think of introspection like tidying up your home—even when it looks clean, dust naturally settles. And if you don't clean or reorganize regularly, things begin to pile up and feel out of place.

In the same way, life's daily chaos can clutter your mind. Introspection helps you clear that emotional dust, reorganize your thoughts, and make sure your actions still align with your values.

As a new mom, introspection becomes even more important. Motherhood floods you with a spectrum of emotions—joy, exhaustion, frustration, deep love, and sometimes even confusion—and that's completely normal.

Instead of letting these feelings overwhelm you, introspection offers a gentle pause—a moment to observe without judgment.

For example, after a sleepless night, you may feel irritated or short-tempered. Instead of blaming yourself, pause and ask:

"Why am I feeling this way? Is it just the lack of sleep? Do I need help, a moment of silence, or simply some rest?"

This small act of self-awareness can shift everything.

It helps you manage stress, respond with intention, and make choices that truly honor your needs.

The Quiet Power of Observation

1. Observer Effect: Did you know that simply observing something can change it? *In the book The Observer Effect,* the author explains how paying attention to something can influence its outcome. When we focus on our emotions, we begin to shift them.

For example, instead of saying, "I'm so stressed," try noticing, "I'm feeling tired because I've had a busy day. Maybe I need rest." Just observing your feelings can change how intense they feel.

2. Remote Viewing: Imagine being stuck in a maze, surrounded by towering walls, unable to find the way out. It feels frustrating and endless.

Now, imagine seeing the maze from above, as if through a drone's perspective. Suddenly, the entire layout becomes clear—you can see where you are and the path forward.

Life's struggles often feel like that maze. Up close, they can seem overwhelming and impossible to navigate. But when you step back and take a broader view, you gain clarity.

This is what introspection does—it helps you see the bigger picture.

It's like looking into a foggy mirror. At first, everything feels blurry and unclear. But instead of judging the reflection, you gently wipe the mirror clean—and, slowly, the image comes into focus. That's the power of observation. It clears the way for the next step: **reflection**—turning awareness into thoughtful action.

Reflection: The Path to Self-Realization

You've just seen the maze from above—clearer now, thanks to the power of observation. But what do you do with that new clarity?

This is where reflection comes in.

When you realize you're stuck in the maze, it's time to pause. Instead of feeling frustrated or banging against the walls, step back—and think about your next move with care. That moment of stepping back is what reflection is all about.

Reflection isn't about criticizing yourself or dwelling on regrets. It's about pausing and asking:

- How am I doing today?
- What's working well for me right now?
- What can I do differently to make things better for myself and my baby?

For new moms, reflection can be a lifeline. Life with a baby is filled with sleepless nights and overwhelming moments, but it's also filled with tiny victories—like your baby's first giggle or the quiet moments when they snuggle close.

Reflection helps you see those moments clearly. It reminds you of your strength, your efforts, and all the love you're pouring into this journey.

It's like stepping back to look at a picture frame. Up close, you only see a few details, but when you take a step back, you notice the beauty of the entire image.

You begin to notice the beauty, the progress, and perhaps the areas that need a little extra care—like more rest or reaching out for support.

When you reflect, something powerful happens: you begin to see that your struggles, your growth, and your love are all connected. This opens the door to something bigger and even deeper—**self-realization.**

The Power of Self-Realization

Self-realization is the moment you realize you're a part of something greater. As a mother, it's understanding that you're not just surviving the maze—you're shaping a life. You were chosen to nurture and guide your baby, and that's not just about biology; it's about purpose.

This realization helps you see that you're stronger and more capable than you think.

A great example of self-realization comes from the book *Autobiography of a Yogi* by Paramahamsa Yoganand. Steve Jobs, the founder of Apple, was deeply inspired by this book. He first read it during a life-changing trip to India, and it remained a part of his life ever since. The book helped him find clarity and purpose.

So powerful was this book that Jobs made it his final message to the world. At his memorial, he made sure everyone who attended received a copy. He wanted to share the wisdom that guided him throughout his life.

For new moms, this book reminds us that self-awareness can change how we see ourselves and our journey. Just like Jobs found strength in it, you too can find the strength to face challenges with grace.

Reflection and self-realization are gifts. They help you grow, honor your challenges, and see the bigger picture. Take a moment today to reflect, and let self-realization help you become the strongest, most compassionate version of yourself—for your baby and for you.

And for me, that transformation became deeply personal.

Realizing that I was chosen for nature's most sacred role—the nurturing of life—completely shifted my identity. I moved from fear to faith, from anxiety to awareness. I stopped resisting and started flowing with the rhythm of life. I wasn't lost; I was finally found—in the arms of nature's grand design.

I became part of something much bigger than myself. My brain rewired not just with knowledge, but with wisdom. In that moment of self-realization, I didn't just heal—I evolved. And in that evolution, I discovered the most powerful truth of all:

I'm not just a person with degrees or achievements. I'm not defined by societal expectations or cultural restrictions.

I am something far greater—a higher self, aligned with nature's divine plan.

I'm not surviving—I'm thriving.

Every moment. Every breath. I am fully alive.

I am nature in motion. I am the creator of life.

I am the flow of life. I am the mother.

And so are you.

This is your true power.

But to awaken it, you must first understand your brain's super-power—neuroplasticity, or adaptability.

Your true power has always been within you, waiting quietly for your awareness to catch up.

And only when you realize this truth—does your real transformation begin.

Once you embrace these tools, it's time to tap into your super-power—**neuroplasticity.**

Your brain is incredibly adaptable right now. This means you have the power to reshape your thoughts, rewire your patterns, and step into the most authentic version of yourself.

It's like chiseling away the extra stone to reveal the masterpiece within. Each mindful thought, each small habit, becomes a stroke that sculpts your brain into its true, vibrant form—full of energy, clarity, and purpose.

So how do you begin? How do you channel this power into your everyday life?

You start by understanding one of the greatest gifts of motherhood: Adaptation—the hidden power that's already working within you.

Adaptation: The Hidden Power of Motherhood

Motherhood is a time when your brain is naturally rewiring itself in ways you may not even realize. It's not just about exhaustion or the emotional rollercoaster—it's about your brain rising to meet the challenge, growing stronger through every moment of adaptation.

Each day, you adjust to your baby's needs—navigating nap schedules, hunger cues, crying spells, and soothing routines—while somehow keeping everything else running.

You do this almost instinctively.

Why?

Because your brain is wired to adapt, and this adaptability is your hidden strength.

Your Brain: In Training Without Even Realizing It

Every time you respond to your baby's needs, juggle responsibilities, or find creative solutions on the spot, your brain is building new neural pathways.

Think of it as a full-body workout—for your mind.

But what if you could channel this same power of adaptation inward?

What if you could train your brain to break free from old habits and emotional patterns?

What if you could let go of inherited fears, outdated beliefs, or the illusion of the status quo that has held you back for too long?

Take Aditi, for example. She carried the heavy weight of her past—until she discovered the power of training her brain. By using the tools and techniques she'd learned and tapping into her brain's peak adaptability, she was able to break free from years of misery. She chose to let go of the pain that had consumed her and embraced the future she had always longed for.

Her story reminds us that change is possible—even when it feels out of reach. And that change begins with the smallest step in a new direction.

Use Your Superpower for You, Too

In the same way, you can use your superpower of adaptability to build habits that nurture your mental and emotional well-being. These small steps may feel challenging at first, especially when life feels chaotic, but over time, they'll make you stronger.

Adaptation is your superpower, mama. You're already using it every day to care for your baby. Now it's time to use it to care for yourself, too.

By following MIRA—Meditation, Introspection, Reflection, and Adaptation—you can train your brain to become more balanced and **holistic**.

MIRA is not just a routine—it's a way to care for your mind and body, helping you thrive as a mom and as yourself.

The journey to your true potential doesn't demand perfection—it simply asks for presence. One mindful breath. One moment of awareness. That's all it takes to begin. You've already taken the first step.

EPILOGUE

This book may end here, but your journey doesn't.

You're not just raising a child—you're rising too.

Your brain is rewiring.

Your heart is stretching.

And you are becoming the mother—and the woman—you were always meant to be.

This isn't just biology. It's transformation.

And it deserves to be recognized.

As humans, we all want to be identified and acknowledged.

Remember this: when you became a mother, the universe itself identified you and acknowledged your importance in keeping the grand plan going.

So, pause. Breathe. Reflect. Keep going.

Not with pressure, but with presence.

Not chasing perfection, but embracing your truth.

Connect with the nurturing energy of Mother Nature to guide you through this journey.

Because every time you choose to show up—for your baby and for yourself—

you're not just surviving motherhood.

You're shaping a brighter, more compassionate world.

Keep going, mama. The world is brighter because of you.

Appendix A

Practical Tools & Takeaways

Chapter 8 – Brain Care for Busy Moms

Time & Energy Management

Key Concepts

- Brain waves change throughout the day; your mental state impacts energy.
- Beta mode burns energy fast (stress, multitasking); balance it with calming states like Alpha or Theta.
- Managing energy is as important as managing time.

Time Tools for Moms

- Time Pockets: Use short gaps for a laugh, breath, or stretch.
- Brain Dump: Write it all out to clear your head.
- Micro Goals: Break tasks into tiny steps—progress over perfection.
- 5-Minute Rule: Do quick tasks right away.

Energy Awareness

- Ask daily:
    - What's fueling me?
    - What's draining me?
    - What's one small shift I can make?

Emotional First Aid Tools

- BOAT Method
    - Breathe
    - Observe without judgment
    - Awareness of emotional layers
    - Tag the emotion

- Scale of Consciousness (Dr. Hawkins)
    - Shift from low-energy states (shame, guilt, fear)
    - Toward high-energy states (love, joy, peace)

Quick Mindful Reset

- Pause
- Breathe deeply
- Ground yourself (touch, senses, presence)
- Let the emotion pass—ride the wave

Remember: Saving time is only useful when you have the energy to use it wisely. Recharge, regulate your emotions, and protect your inner peace.

Chapter 9 – Mommy Brain Boosters

Simple Hacks to Thrive as a New Mom

Brain Fuel & Hacks

- Eat brain-friendly foods: walnuts, avocados, berries, omega-3s.
- Keep your brain active with stories, podcasts, puzzles, journaling etc.
- Stay socially connected—talk with family, friends, or mom groups. Express your emotions.
- Hydrate well and take short naps when possible.

Gut Health: Your Second Brain

- Eat fiber-rich, balanced meals with probiotics (yogurt, garlic) and prebiotics (bananas, asparagus).
- Drink plenty of water and limit processed sugar.
- Practice mindful eating—chew slowly and savor your food.
- Quality sleep supports gut health and overall mood.

Sleep Hacks

- Nap when the baby naps.
- Create a calming bedtime routine and limit screen time before bed.
- Keep your room cool and dark; avoid caffeine late in the day.

- Share night feedings to get longer rest stretches.
- Use relaxation techniques and white noise.

Heart-Brain Coherence

- Practice heart-focused breathing and cultivate positive emotions.
- Use gratitude journaling and spend time in nature.
- Connect deeply with your baby through shared quiet moments.

Building New Habits

- Repeat routines consistently to create automatic habits.
- Use visual reminders and simplify tasks.
- Celebrate small wins and seek support from others.

Mind & Body Hacks

- Use sound or humming to improve focus.
- Practice positive affirmations and creative outlets.
- Wear comfortable clothing and incorporate babywearing.
- Move gently with stretches, stroller walks, or baby yoga.

The Power of Laughter

- Laughter releases feel-good hormones and reduces stress.
- Share humor to build stronger bonds with family and your baby.
- Use laughter as a tool for healing and emotional resilience.

Remember: Nourish your brain, gut, and heart with good food, restful sleep, and positive habits. Stay connected, practice kindness to yourself, and never underestimate the healing power of laughter. Small daily steps build a strong foundation for thriving motherhood.

Chapter 10 – The 5 Golden Rules for Brain Health

1. Balance: Find Your Sweet Spot

- Balance effort and rest to keep your brain calm and clear.
- Notice when you're stressed and take moments to breathe and reset.

2. Hormonal Harmony: Manage Your Brain Chemistry

- Understand how dopamine drives desires and habits.
- Practice gentle "dopamine detoxes" by stepping back from constant stimulation (social media, shopping).
- Aim to regain control and focus on what truly nourishes you.

3. Remove Mental Barriers: Conquer Your Mental Monsters

- Identify limiting beliefs and self-doubt.
- Challenge old thoughts and replace them with positive, empowering ones.
- Progress is gradual—embrace the journey of mindset transformation.

4. Learn to Say 'No': Protect Your Energy

- Saying 'no' is a powerful act of self-care.
- Set boundaries to avoid overwhelm and burnout.
- Use honesty and kindness when declining requests.
- Pause and evaluate what truly supports your well-being.

5. The Art of Letting Go: Clear Mental Clutter

- Release thoughts and habits that no longer serve you.
- Make space for growth, peace, and new experiences.
- Like pruning a garden, letting go helps your brain grow stronger and healthier.

Remember: Balance effort with rest, manage your hormones and mindset, set clear boundaries, and let go of what no longer serves you. These simple yet powerful rules protect your brain and nurture your well-being as a thriving mom.

Chapter 11 – Unlock Your True Potential (MIRA Framework)

1. Meditation: Calm and Clarity

- Use deep breathing to shift from busy to restful brain states.
- Visualize your goals and practice positive affirmations.
- Avoid negativity to protect your emotional well-being.
- Your calmness positively influences your baby through mirror neurons.

2. Introspection: Self-Awareness

- Check in with your body and emotions regularly.
- Observe thoughts without judgment to gain clarity.
- Step back to see the bigger picture and understand your needs.

3. Reflection: Thoughtful Action

- Pause to evaluate what's working and what needs change.
- Celebrate small victories and learn from challenges.
- Use reflection to align your actions with your values and goals.

4. Adaptation: Embrace Change and Growth

- Recognize your brain's natural ability to adapt and form new habits.
- Use this adaptability to build healthier, stronger mental and emotional patterns.
- Practice patience—growth happens with consistent effort over time.

Quick Summary:

MIRA

- Meditation for calm and focus
- Introspection for awareness
- Reflection for clarity and alignment
- Adaptation for growth and resilience

Use these four steps to unlock your true potential and thrive in motherhood and beyond.

Remember: Embrace the MIRA framework—Meditate, Introspect, Reflect, and Adapt—to unlock your inner strength, nurture your growth, and thrive as both a mother and your true self.

Appendix B

References and Recommended Readings

Ahsan, A., Nadeem, A., Habib, A., Basaria, A. A. A., Tariq, R., & Raufi, N. (2023). Post-traumatic stress disorder following childbirth: A neglected cause. Frontiers in Global Women's Health.

Alehagen, S., Wijma, K., Lundberg, U., Melin, B., & Wijma, B. (2001). Catecholamine and cortisol reaction to childbirth. International Journal of Behavioral Medicine, 8(1), 50–65.

Armour, J. A. (1991). The little brain in the heart. In M. Sibinga (Ed.), Heart and soul: The impact of emotion on health (pp. 69–78). Harwood Academic Publishers.

Athan, A. M. (2024). A critical need for the concept of matrescence in perinatal psychiatry. Frontiers in Psychiatry, 15, 1364845.

Bailey, M. T., & Coe, C. L. (1999). Maternal separation disrupts the integrity of the intestinal microflora in infant rhesus monkeys. Developmental Psychobiology, 35(2), 146–155.

Barba-Müller, E., Sosa, F. M., & Garcia, A. P. (2019). Matrescence: The psychological and emotional changes of motherhood. Journal of Women's Health, 28(8), 1061–1067.

Belkaid, Y., & Hand, T. W. (2014). Role of the microbiota in immunity and inflammation. Cell, 157(1), 121–141.

Benedict, C., Vogel, H., Jonas, W., Woting, A., Blaut, M., Schürmann, A., & Cedernaes, J. (2012). Gut microbiota and sleep-wake regulation. Current Opinion in Clinical Nutrition & Metabolic Care, 15(6), 571–577.

Brizendine, L. (2006). The Female Brain. Morgan Road Books.

Champagne, F. A., & Meaney, M. J. (2006). Stress during pregnancy alters maternal behavior in the rat. Journal of Neuroendocrinology, 18(7), 493–502.

Chopra, D. (1994). The seven spiritual laws of success. Amber-Allen Publishing.

Courtwright, D. T. (2019). The age of addiction: How bad habits became big business. Harvard University Press.

Cryan, J. F., O'Riordan, K. J., Cowan, C. S. M., Sandhu, K. V., Bastiaanssen, T. F. S., Boehme, M., … & Dinan, T. G. (2019). The microbiota-gut-brain axis. Physiological Reviews, 99(4), 1877–2013.

Davies, S. J., et al. (2025). Cognitive function decline in pregnancy and postpartum: A meta-analysis. BMC Pregnancy and Childbirth.

Davies, S. J., Seguin, J. A., & Sokolowski, H. M. (2021). Cognitive changes during pregnancy: Memory and language impairments. Scientific Reports, 11, 12543.

Dispenza, J. (2012). Breaking the habit of being yourself: How to lose your mind and create a new one. Hay House.

Dispenza, J. (2014). You Are the Placebo: Making Your Mind Matter. Hay House.

Dunsworth, H. M., Warrener, A. G., Deacon, T., Ellison, P. T., & Pontzer, H. (2012). Metabolic hypothesis for human altriciality. Proceedings of the National Academy of Sciences, 109(38), 15212–15216.

Dunkel Schetter, C., & Tanner, L. (2012). Anxiety, depression and stress in pregnancy: Implications for mothers, children, research, and practice. Current Opinion in Psychiatry, 25(2), 141–148.

Eagleman, D. (2015). The brain: The story of you. Pantheon Books.

Eisenberger, N. I. (2012). The pain of social disconnection: Examining the shared neural underpinnings of physical and social pain. Nature Reviews Neuroscience, 13(6), 421–434.

Feldman, R., Gordon, I., & Zagoory-Sharon, O. (2007). Maternal–paternal bonding and the effects of oxytocin in humans. Hormones and Behavior, 52(3), 458–465.

Gegenfurtner, K. R., & Blakemore, C. (2015). The dress: A color constancy illusion. Perception, 44(10), 1173–1181.

Goldman, J., & Goldman, A. (2017). The Humming Effect: Sound Healing for health and happiness. Healing Arts Press.

Harari, Y. N. (2015). Sapiens: A brief history of humankind. HarperCollins.

Hawkins, D. R. (2020). The map of consciousness explained: A proven energy scale to actualize your ultimate potential. Hay House.

Hoekzema, E., Barba-Müller, E., Pozzobon, C., Picado, M., Lucco, F., García-García, D., Soliva, J. C., Tobeña, A., Desco, M., Crone, E. A., Ballesteros, A., Carmona, S., & Vilarroya, O. (2017). Pregnancy leads to long-lasting changes in human brain structure. Nature Neuroscience, 20(2), 287–296.

Huberman, A. (2021). How light affects your brain and body [Audio podcast episode]. Huberman Lab Podcast.

Huberman, A. (2021). Using NSDR (Non-Sleep Deep Rest) for enhancing learning. Huberman Lab Podcast.

Isaacson, W. (2011). Steve Jobs. Simon & Schuster.

Jones, N. (2022). The observer effect (Joseph Bridgeman Series, Book 3). Blackstone Publishing.

Kahneman, D. (2011). Thinking, fast and slow. Farrar, Straus and Giroux.

Kim, P. (2016). Maternal brain and behavior: The influence of pregnancy and early motherhood on the human brain. Brain Research, 1642, 227–234.

Lakhiani, V. (2016). The code of the extraordinary mind: 10 unconventional laws to redefine your life and succeed on your own terms. Rodale Books.

Lembke, A. (2021). Dopamine nation: Finding balance in the age of indulgence. Dutton.

Lipton, B. H. (2005). The biology of belief: Unleashing the power of consciousness, matter & miracles. Hay House.

Lonstein, J. S., & Gammie, S. C. (2002). Sensory, hormonal, and neural control of maternal aggression in laboratory rodents. Neuroscience & Biobehavioral Reviews, 26(8), 869–888.

Lupien, S. J., McEwen, B. S., Gunnar, M. R., & Heim, C. (2009). Effects of stress throughout the lifespan on the brain, behaviour and cognition. Nature Reviews Neuroscience, 10(6), 434–445.

MacLean, P. D. (1990). The triune brain in evolution: Role in paleocerebral functions. Springer.

Marlin, B. J., Mitre, M., D'Amour, J. A., Chao, M. V., & Froemke, R. C. (2015). Oxytocin enables maternal behaviour by balancing cortical inhibition. Nature, 520, 499–504.

Maté, G. (2004). Hold on to your kids: Why parents need to matter more than peers. Vintage Canada.

Maté, G. (2019). The myth of normal: Trauma, illness, and healing in a toxic culture. Avery.

Mayer, E. A. (2016). The mind-gut connection. Harper Wave.

McCraty, R., Bradley, R. T., & Tomasino, D. (2015). Science of the heart, Volume 2: Exploring the role of the heart in human performance. HeartMath Institute.

McCraty, R., Deyhle, A., & Childre, D. (2018). Global study of human heart rhythm synchronization with the Earth's time-varying magnetic field. Journal of Behavioral and Brain Science, 8(6), 85–95.

McGuff, D., & Little, J. (2009). Body by science: A research-based program for strength training, bodybuilding, and complete fitness in 12 minutes a week. McGraw-Hill.

Murphy, J. (1963). The power of your subconscious mind. Prentice Hall.

Nestor, J. (2020). Breath: The new science of a lost art. Riverhead Books.

O'Connor, M.-F., Palitsky, R., Wilson, D. T., Friedman, S. E., Ruiz, J. M., Sullivan, D., & Allen, J. J. B. (2023). The relationship of prolonged grief disorder symptoms with hemodynamic response to grief recall among bereaved adults. Psychosomatic Medicine, 85(6), 545–550.

Orchard, E. R., Rutherford, H. J. V., Holmes, A. J., & Jamadar, S. (2023). Matrescence: Lifetime impact of motherhood on cognition and the brain. Trends in Cognitive Sciences, 27(3), 302–316.

Perls, F. S., Hefferline, R. F., & Goodman, P. (1994). Gestalt therapy: Excitement and growth in the human personality. The Gestalt Journal Press.

Pert, C. B. (1997). Molecules of emotion: Why you feel the way you feel. Scribner.

Psychology Today. (2022, June 21). How the brain's mirror neurons affect empathy.

Qin, J., Li, R., Raes, J., Arumugam, M., Burgdorf, K. S., Manichanh, C., … & Wang, J. (2010). A human gut microbial gene catalogue established by metagenomic sequencing. Nature, 464(7285), 59–65.

Raphael, D. (1973). The Tender Gift: Breastfeeding. Schocken Books.

Rizzolatti, G., & Sinigaglia, C. (2008). Mirrors in the brain: How our minds share actions and emotions. Oxford University Press.

Roberson, D., Davidoff, J., & Shapiro, L. R. (2000). Color categories are not universal: Evidence from the Himba of Namibia. Cognition, 75(1), 1–10.

Sacks, A. (2018). A new way to think about the transition to motherhood [TED Talk].

Shonkoff, J. P., Garner, A. S., Siegel, B. S., Dobbins, M. I., Earls, M. F., McGuinn, L., … & Wood, D. L. (2012). The lifelong effects of early childhood adversity and toxic stress. Pediatrics, 129(1), e232–e246.

Siegel, D. J., & Bryson, T. P. (2012). The whole-brain child: 12 revolutionary strategies to nurture your child's developing mind. Delacorte Press.

Swain, J. E., Lorberbaum, J. P., Kose, S., & Strathearn, L. (2011). Brain basis of early parent-infant interactions. Journal of Child Psychology and Psychiatry, 48(3–4), 262–287.

Tsabary, S. (2010). The conscious parent: Transforming ourselves, empowering our children. Namaste Publishing.

Vox Media. (2019). The mind explained [TV series episode: "Mindfulness"]. Netflix.

Walker, M. (2017). Why we sleep: The New Science of Sleep and Dreams. Penguin Books.

Winfrey, O. (Host). (1997, February 17). The Oprah Winfrey Show [TV series episode]. Harpo Productions.

World Health Organization. (2023). More than a third of women experience lasting health problems after childbirth. Geneva: World Health Organization.

Yehuda, R., & Bierer, L. M. (2009). The relevance of epigenetics to PTSD: Implications for the DSM-V. Journal of Traumatic Stress, 22(5), 427–434.

Yogananda, P. (2004). Autobiography of a yogi. Self-Realization Fellowship. (Original work published 1946)

Zahariades, D. (2017). The art of saying no. Independently published.

Zheng, Y., et al. (2018). Decreased spontaneous neural activity in postpartum women. Frontiers in Psychology.

Appendix C

Glossary

A

Amygdala: A small almond-shaped region deep in the brain that plays a key role in processing emotions like fear, anxiety, and attachment.

Attachment: The deep emotional connection formed between individuals, especially a caregiver and child, which shapes emotional and social development.

Abscission: The natural detachment of plant parts, such as leaves, fruits, or flowers, typically to support growth or reproduction. Metaphorically, it illustrates the brain's process of pruning unused neural connections and letting go of unnecessary memories while preserving important lessons.

B

Baby-Proofing the Brain: A metaphor for mentally and emotionally preparing for the challenges of parenting, particularly in early motherhood.

Banker Brain: A playful term for a mindset shaped by banking experience—focused on order, logic, efficiency, and financial thinking.

Biological Marvel: A phrase celebrating the complexity and wonder of the human body or brain, especially in motherhood.

BOAT Technique: A method to understand and manage emotions using four steps: Breathe, Observe, Aware, and Tag the emotion.

Boss Brain: A term referring to the heart's neural network—often called the "little brain"—which influences brain activity and plays a key role in guiding emotion, intuition, and decision-making.

Brain Care: The loving practice of nurturing your mental and emotional well-being through restful sleep, mindfulness, and compassionate support.

Brain Dump: A method of writing down all thoughts to declutter the mind and improve focus or emotional processing.

Brain Fog: A mental state characterized by confusion, forgetfulness, and difficulty concentrating, often linked to fatigue or hormonal changes.

Brain Hijack: When strong emotions, like fear or anger, override rational thinking and lead to impulsive responses.

Brain Rewiring: The brain's ability to change its structure and connections in response to new experiences, learning, or healing.

Brain Waves: Rhythmic electrical patterns in the brain that vary with states like alertness, relaxation, or sleep.

C

Cognitive Behavioral Therapy (CBT): A psychological treatment that helps individuals identify and change unhelpful thought patterns and behaviors.

Conditioned Brain: The part of the brain shaped by repeated experiences and learned responses—often from childhood—that often operates on autopilot.

Conscious Neural Pruning: The intentional letting go of old thought patterns or habits, much like the brain naturally trims unused connections.

Cortisol: A hormone released during stress that affects energy levels, mood, and memory—important in the body's stress response.

Cosmic Womb: A deeply nurturing space associated with creation, renewal, and inner transformation—evoking a sense of emotional and spiritual emergence.

D

Dementia: A progressive condition marked by decline in memory, thinking, and reasoning, affecting daily life and independence.

DHA-Rich Food: Foods high in docosahexaenoic acid, an omega-3 fatty acid vital for brain development and function.

Dopamine: A chemical messenger in the brain that influences motivation, pleasure, and the brain's reward system.

Dopamine Detox: A practice of reducing overstimulation—like from social media or sugar—to reset the brain's reward sensitivity.

E

Epigenetics: The science of how behaviors and environmental influences can affect how genes are expressed, turning them on or off without altering the underlying DNA.

Executive Function: High-level brain skills such as decision-making, attention control, and impulse regulation.

F

Fight, Flight, or Freeze Response: The body's automatic survival mechanism that kicks in during stress or perceived danger.

G

Gut-Brain Axis: A two-way communication system between the brain and digestive tract that influences mood, stress, and immunity.

Gestalt: A concept describing an organized whole that is perceived as more than the sum of its individual parts.

H

Heart-Brain Coherence: A physiological state where the brain and heart rhythms sync, promoting clarity, calm, and emotional well-being.

Homeostasis: The body's ability to maintain internal balance and stability despite external changes.

Holistic Brain: A view of the brain as interconnected with body, emotions, and environment—not just a thinking organ.

L

Limbic Capitalism: A term suggesting modern marketing targets our emotional brain to drive behavior and consumption.

Laughter Doctor: A playful concept or person who promotes healing through humor and joyful connection.

Logical Magic and Magical Logic: A poetic way to describe the brain's blend of scientific function and mysterious creativity.

M

Matrescence: The physical, emotional, and psychological transition a woman undergoes as she becomes a mother—similar in scope to adolescence.

Melatonin (Vampire Hormone): A hormone that regulates sleep, often called the "vampire hormone" because it is released in darkness.

Mental Makeover: A shift in mindset or thinking patterns aimed at improving emotional well-being and mental clarity.

Mental Metro Line: A metaphor for the brain's complex network of thoughts and pathways, guiding how we think and feel.

Mental Monsters: Unhelpful thoughts, fears, or inner critics that disrupt peace of mind or emotional growth.

Microbiota: The community of beneficial microbes in the gut, which play a key role in digestion, immunity, and brain health.

Mirror Neurons: Special brain cells that activate both when we act and when we observe others—underpinning empathy and connection.

Mom Guilt: A common emotional experience where mothers feel they are not doing enough or failing in some aspect of parenting.

Momfluencer: A term for mothers who influence others through social media by sharing parenting, lifestyle, or wellness content.

Mommy Brain: A term used to describe the cognitive changes—such as forgetfulness or emotional sensitivity—often experienced during pregnancy or postpartum.

Mother Molecules: A poetic term for key hormones and neurotransmitters, like oxytocin, that play a central role in caregiving and bonding.

Mother Wound: Deep emotional pain stemming from unmet needs in childhood, often inherited across generations.

Muggle Brain: A light-hearted reference to a more rational or conventional way of thinking, lacking intuitive or imaginative flair.

Master Storyteller: A metaphor for the brain's ability to create and interpret meaning through internal narratives and memories.

N

Neural Pathways: The brain's communication routes that strengthen with repeated thoughts, actions, or behaviors.

Neuroplasticity: The brain's remarkable ability to reorganize and form new connections in response to learning or experience.

Neurons: The fundamental cells of the nervous system that transmit information through electrical and chemical signals.

O

Observer Effect: The idea that observing one's thoughts or emotions can influence or change them, fostering self-awareness.

Oxytocin: Often called the "love hormone," it supports bonding, trust, and emotional connection—especially during childbirth and breastfeeding.

P

Placebo Effect: A beneficial response to a treatment that occurs because of belief in its effectiveness, even if the treatment is inactive.

Postpartum Depression (PPD): A serious mood disorder that can affect women after childbirth, involving sadness, fatigue, and difficulty bonding.

Prefrontal Cortex: The brain's front region responsible for decision-making, planning, and self-regulation.

Pseudo-Stress: A state of perceived but not actual danger, which can trigger the stress response unnecessarily.

R

Reel-istic vs Real-istic: Terms highlighting the contrast between curated social media content ("reels") and the often-messy reality of everyday life.

Remote Viewing: The practice of mentally stepping back to observe a situation from a broader perspective, gaining clarity by seeing the bigger picture.

S

Scale of Consciousness: A model that ranks emotions and states of being by vibrational energy—from low (shame) to high (love, peace).

Second Brain: A nickname for the gut, due to its vast neural network and strong influence on mood and cognition.

Sleep Deprivation: A lack of sufficient sleep, which can impair memory, mood, and overall brain function—especially common in early parenting.

Stress Hormones: Chemicals like cortisol and adrenaline released in response to stress, affecting physical and emotional states.

Subconscious Brain / Mind: The part of the mind that operates below conscious awareness, storing beliefs, memories, and patterns that influence thoughts, emotions, and behaviors.

Sympathetic and Parasympathetic Nervous Systems: Two branches of the autonomic nervous system—one activates the body during stress, the other calms it.

System 1 & 2 Thinking: A model of thought where System 1 is fast and intuitive, and System 2 is slow and analytical.

T

Theta State: A brainwave frequency associated with deep relaxation, insight, and emotional healing—often accessed during meditation.

Time Pockets: Small windows of uninterrupted time used for self-care, reflection, or focused attention.

V

Visualization: A mental practice of forming clear, purposeful images or scenarios in the mind to support emotional healing, focus, or the achievement of desired outcomes.

W

Whole Brain Regulation: A balanced engagement of all brain regions, promoting emotional stability and cognitive flexibility.

3-Pound Wizard (Brain): A term that refers to the human brain—small in size but remarkably powerful, creative, and complex.

Y

Yoga Nidra: A deeply restful meditative state between wakefulness and sleep that supports relaxation, emotional balance, and neurological healing.

About the Author

Prashanthi Punyakoti is a writer and a former banker. With a background in biotechnology and years of experience in the banking sector, she stepped away from her career following a pregnancy loss and an unexpected new beginning.

As she cared for her infant—while coping with grief, identity shifts, financial strain, and the unspoken challenges of early motherhood—she began exploring the science of the maternal brain.

What began as a personal science quest for her own questions led her to understand the maternal brain not only in a scientific way but in a holistic way—through the lens of emotion, experience, and transformation. As she slowly began to heal, her curiosity deepened into compassion—a heartfelt longing to support other new moms who feel lost, and to help them rediscover their strength, clarity, and sense of self on the path to healing and growth.

Her writing blends neuroscience, holistic wellness, and heartfelt storytelling to create compassionate resources for mothers who often feel unseen, unheard, or overwhelmed.

When she's not writing, Prashanthi enjoys journaling, singing, dancing, and finding beauty in life's small, mindful moments. Moms & Brains is her first book.

Notes

Notes

Notes

www.ingramcontent.com/pod-product-compliance
Ingram Content Group UK Ltd.
Pitfield, Milton Keynes, MK11 3LW, UK
UKHW041313190726
13845UKWH00025B/226

9 789334 276626